University of Michigan Business School Management Series

INNOVATIVE SOLUTIONS TO THE
PRESSING PROBLEMS OF BUSINESS

The mission of the University of Michigan Business School Management Series is to provide accessible, practical, and cutting-edge solutions to the most critical challenges facing businesspeople today. The UMBS Management Series provides concepts and tools for people who seek to make a significant difference in their organizations. Drawing on the research and experience of faculty at the University of Michigan Business School, the books are written to stretch thinking while providing practical, focused, and innovative solutions to the pressing problems of business.

Also available in the UMBS series:

Becoming a Better Value Creator, by Anjan V. Thakor

Achieving Success Through Social Capital, by Wayne Baker

Improving Customer Satisfaction, Loyalty, and Profit,
by Michael D. Johnson and Anders Gustafsson

The Compensation Solution, by John E. Tropman

Strategic Interviewing, by Richaurd Camp, Mary Vielhaber,
and Jack L. Simonetti

Creating the Multicultural Organization, by Taylor Cox

For additional information on any of these titles or future
titles in the series, visit www.umbsbooks.com.

Executive Summary

Organizations around the world are experiencing unprecedented levels of competitive pressure in the global marketplace of the twenty-first century. This competition is causing organizations in every segment of the economy to place a greater emphasis on improving their performance (financial, operating, service, quality, and innovation). This emphasis on improved performance manifests itself in a very simple organizational reality: managers at all levels must become more proficient at getting desired results to keep their jobs and to keep their careers on track. And the organizational mandate for improved performance and better results is a never-ending cycle.

An essential question must be asked by managers operating under this mandate: What do I need to do to get better results? In this book, we explore the answer to this critical question based on the input of over two thousand "high-performance managers" in nearly every type of organization you can imagine. The findings from this applied research show that results-oriented managers place a tremendous emphasis on creating a workplace that brings out the best in people while simultaneously developing effective systems and processes that improve performance.

Every manager can improve performance by building a model of key practices that support getting results. This book shows managers how to do this, guiding them through what we have come to call the "five absolutes" of high performance. These absolutes, based on the input of managers in our study, are critical management practices that are necessary for eliciting high performance and getting results.

We explore the keys to managerial career success and survival (Chapter One) and make a strong case for the necessity of improving your personal performance as a manager. After this we begin our exploration of the key absolutes by demonstrating the importance of creating an appropriate focus on results for you and your operation (Chapter Two) and how to go about equipping your operation for high performance (Chapter Three). Critical practices for developing a results-oriented workplace (Chapter Four) and for creating people performance power (Chapter Five) are reviewed for your personal application. Finally, we share what managers in this study considered to be the secret to long-term success: the ongoing renewal of your processes, people, and yourself as a professional and human being (Chapter Six). This journey is interactive, with a serious emphasis on application and implementation, to help you develop the practices and habits possessed by high-performing managers.

Getting Results

Five Absolutes for
High Performance

Clinton O. Longenecker
and Jack L. Simonetti

 JOSSEY-BASS
A Wiley Company
San Francisco

Published by Jossey-Bass
A Wiley Imprint
989 Market Street, San Francisco, CA 94103-1741   www.josseybass.com

Jossey-Bass books and products are available through most bookstores. To contact Jossey-Bass directly call our Customer Care Department within the U.S. at 800-956-7739, outside the U.S. at 317-572-3986 or fax 317-572-4002.

Jossey-Bass also publishes its books in a variety of electronic formats. Some content that appears in print may not be available in electronic books.

Library of Congress Cataloging-in-Publication Data

Longenecker, Clinton O., date.
    Getting results: five absolutes for high performance/Clinton O. Longenecker, Jack L. Simonetti.
        p. cm. — (University of Michigan Business School management series)
    Includes bibliographical references and index.
    ISBN 0-7879-5388-1 (alk. paper) ISBN 978-1-119-18533-8 (paperback)
    1. Organizational effectiveness. 2. Organizational behavior. 3. Total quality management. I. Simonetti, Jack L. II. Title. III. Series.
    HD58.9 .L665 2001
    658.4—dc21   2001029328

FIRST EDITION
HB Printing   10 9 8 7 6
PB Printing 10 9 8 7 6 5 4 3 2 1

Contents

We'd like to dedicate this book to

My beloved wife and best friend for life, Cindy;
my children, Clint, Shannon, and Steve; my parents,
Clint Jr. and Rita; and my in-laws, Chuck and Ginny
Breese; all of whom have taught me the importance
of faith, people, integrity, and passion.

My wife, Judy, a super mom and grandmother; my
children, Lynn, Mark, Terri, and Paul, and their spouses;
my wonderful grandchildren; and my parents and family
for all their help and support.

Series Foreword

Welcome to the University of Michigan Business School Management Series. The books in this series address the most urgent problems facing business today. The series is part of a larger initiative at The University of Michigan Business School (UMBS) that ties together a range of efforts to create and share knowledge through conferences, survey research, interactive and distance training, print publications, and new media

It is just this type of broad-based initiative that sparked my love affair with UMBS in 1984. From the day I arrived I was enamored with the quality of the research, the quality of the MBA program, and the quality of the Executive Education Center. Here was a business school committed to new lines of research, new ways of teaching, and the practical application of ideas. It was a place where innovative thinking could result in tangible outcomes.

The UMBS Management Series is one very important outcome, and it has an interesting history. It turns out that every year five thousand participants in our executive program fill out a marketing survey in which they write statements indicating the most important problems they face. One day Lucy Chin, one of our administrators, handed me a document containing all these statements. A content analysis of the data resulted in a list of forty-five pressing problems. The topics ranged from growing a company to managing personal stress. The list covered a wide territory, and I started to see its potential. People in organizations tend to be driven by a very traditional set of problems, but the solutions evolve. I went to my friends at Jossey-Bass to discuss a publishing project. The discussion eventually grew into the University of Michigan Business School Management Series— Innovative Solutions to the Pressing Problems of Business.

The books are independent of each other, but collectively they create a comprehensive set of management tools that cut across all the functional areas of business—from strategy to human resources to finance, accounting, and operations. They draw on the interdisciplinary research of the Michigan faculty. Yet each book is written so a serious manager can read it quickly and act immediately. I think you will find that they are books that will make a significant difference to you and your organization.

Robert E. Quinn, Consulting Editor
M.E. Tracy Distinguished Professor
University of Michigan Business School

Preface

Our goal in this book is straightforward but absolutely essential—to get you to think about your current managerial strengths and limitations and how to build on both to increase your performance and propensity for getting better results. In the words of one very successful financial services executive, "Things are so hectic and fast-paced at work these days that it is easy to think about everything but myself as a manager . . . what I am doing and how well I am doing it . . . I know that if I don't stop and take time to seriously think about these things my performance will suffer rather than improve and so will my ability to get results."

To accomplish its goal, this book builds on twenty years of research and experience dedicated to why modern organizations and managers fail and why they succeed. We have had the privilege of working in, consulting with, and studying some of the very best organizations in the world in a diverse group of industries. We have done the same with organizations that were struggling to find their way and even, in some cases, near death. We have seen overwhelming achievement and success and all the trappings and energy that come with operating in the stratosphere. And we have personally witnessed and experienced the frustration, anxiety, anger, and even devastation brought on by organizational and managerial failure.

All these experiences have a common denominator: there is a major difference between good and bad managers and the organizations that they create and lead, and that major difference revolves around who is doing a better job of getting results by implementing the most basic of all management practices. These fundamental practices always have a dual focus in that they require managers to demonstrate excellence on a personal level in their approach to running their operations and at the same time to demonstrate the ability to work effectively with and through their people to get things done. We would go so far as to say that managers wishing to get better results must demonstrate high performance in both these key areas or their careers may be derailed.

Thus we believe that organizations and managers need to become more results-oriented in their approach to doing business today. And we strongly believe that managers are ultimately responsible for performing value-added actions that help please their customers and create shareholder value. Tremendous pressure for better results exists because of the ultra-competitive global marketplace and unprecedented levels of change. This pressure has created tremendous demand for managers and leaders who know how to think and lead their operations and people forward in an appropriate fashion. This book will help you improve your ability to get results by providing you with research findings, case studies, self-assessments, interactive exercises, and practical advice drawn from the world in which you operate as a manager.

■ Who This Book Is For

This book is for managers of all levels who are looking for ways to improve the performance not only of themselves but also of the people they are directly responsible for. For example, if you are a new manager, this book can serve as a guide for developing a game plan to become a complete results–oriented manager. If you're a seasoned manager, you can use this book to assess and review your current managerial practices and determine which ones need improvement to enhance your ability to get results. If you're a senior-level executive, entrepreneur, or consultant, you can use the results-oriented practices described in this book as a benchmark for developing a high-performance management team or as a strategy to create a more high-performance organization. If you are interested in improving your own management performance as well as adding value to your organization, you will find practical and applicable practices and ideas in this book that will improve your performance and the performance of your people.

■ How This Book Is Organized

Although this book is based on extensive research, it is organized for the business community rather than to provide a basis for further academic work. Chapter One defines and illustrates the theme this book is addressing: that to improve your performance as a manager, it is essential to have a passionate commitment to the management absolutes necessary for improvement and success. This commitment must be coupled with the earnest realization that personal improvement is not optional but rather an organizational imperative for career survival and success today. The remaining five chapters provide tools, skills, and interactive exercises designed to show you how high-performing managers improve their performance and get better results:

1. Get everyone on the same page: Focus on the purpose of your organization.
2. Prepare for battle: Equip your operation with tools, talent, and technology.

3. Stoke the fire of performance: Create a climate for results.
4. Build bridges on the road to results: Nurture relationships with people.
5. Keep the piano in tune: Practice continuous renewal.

Your ability to think through the concepts presented here, answer the questions posed in the exercises, and apply these five management absolutes to both your professional and personal life will help determine your return on investment for reading this book.

■ Acknowledgments

We want to thank Bob Quinn for his vision in and leadership on the UMSB Management Series and for his willingness to make us part of this outstanding team. We want to praise the efforts of the great Jossey-Bass team, specifically Cedric Crocker and Byron Schneider, who both know how to get results. A special thanks to Jeanne Woodward of Bergez & Woodward and copyeditor Hilary Powers, whose input and guidance in the creation and completion of this book were both invaluable and greatly appreciated.

We want to thank the countless organizations that have opened their doors to us in our ongoing research pursuits over the years. We also want to thank the countless managers who have opened their minds to us and who willingly shared their time, experience, and wisdom in this large research project. This effort would have been impossible without them.

We would also like to thank a very special group of leaders who practice the age-old principle described in Proverbs 27:17, "As iron sharpens iron, so one person can sharpen another." Thank you for helping to sharpen us: Sonny Ariss (a sounding board and support); Melanie Barnett (a consummate professional); Tom Dobb (an innovative manager); Dave Ellison (an admiral in the U.S. Navy and an excellent role model to many);

Denny Gioia (a wonderful mentor); Tim Iorio (a man of great faith); Jim Jones (a strong leader); Dave Lahote (a real teacher); Paul Longenecker (a strong man); Richard Longenecker (a driver); Tom Moore (a successful techno-manager); Chuck Ostermyer (a real change agent); Mike Parker (a learned professional); John Passante (a man on a mission); Gary Pinkel (a great coach); Kris Garber Rodgers (a very positive professional); Joe Scazzero (a quantitative wizard); Debbie Schaefer (a ground breaker); Hank Sims (who planted seeds); Jim Staley (a visionary leader); Tim Stansfield (an outstanding entrepreneurial engineer); Joe Straka and Joe Sass (good friends); Bob Tobey (a real team builder); Lee Tooman (a profound thinker); and Dr. George Van Buren (a life saver).

Several years ago we lost a dear friend named Jan Babcock to cancer at age thirty-five. We had the opportunity to be the last to talk to her, a few hours before she slipped into a coma and passed away. Jan's final words were "Keep loving your wife, take care of your kids, and keep your priorities straight. . . . I am very tired now and it is time for me to sleep." Jan was very effective in getting great results in every area of her life as evidenced by the fact that she was a great person on earth as a wife, mother of five children, friend, and professional, and we believe that these words are part of her legacy.

Finally, we would like a special thanks to Dolores Lucitte, Shirley Lively, and Sandy Whitman, whose professionalism and performance enable us to do what we do and to do it well. And we would also like to thank Barbara, Joanna, Paige, Linda, and Amy of the Harvest Lane–Lucas County Public Library for support and encouragement in this effort. And to Michelle Wolff for all her great work on the home stretch. Getting results is always a team effort!

April 2001   Clinton O. Longenecker
Toledo, Ohio   Jack L. Simonetti

Getting Results

The Call for Results

everal years ago, we conducted an executive education program with a group of senior managers in a growing service organization. In a serious discussion of what factors they considered to be most important to their career success, a heated debate broke out. Opinions were strong and varied about how to keep your job and get ahead. All the executives seemed to have their favorite three or four success factors that they championed during this discussion. Here are some of the typical opinions that emerged from this energized exchange:

"Be sure to take care of the bottom line."
"It all comes back to who you know and your connections."

"You've got to be willing to pay the price."
"Get as much cross-functional experience as you can."
"Find a mentor to help show you the way."
"Surround yourself with the best people possible."
"You've got to keep improving yourself."
"Get your systems and processes working in concert."
"Get involved in high-profile projects."
"Be willing and able to make the difficult decisions."

The passion, interest, and energy generated by this discussion encouraged us to explore this critically important career issue in greater depth since these views were only opinions at this point. To do this, we conducted a formal survey of more than 5,000 managers all across the United States. Top, middle, and front-line managers were surveyed from nearly every major U.S. industry, including high tech, chemical, health care, automotive, banking, financial services, steel, retail, telecommunications, and transportation. In this study, managers were asked to identify and rank order the factors they considered to be most important to their personal career survival and success. *Stop right now and on a sheet of paper list the top five most important factors that you feel are essential for your career survival and success in your current situation.*

If you are like the managers in our study, getting better results is most likely on your list in some way, shape, or form.[1] Although some variance exists across organizations, industries, and management levels, people completing this survey made it very clear that getting results is almost always the most critical career survival and success factor and the name of the career game.

The CEO of a *Fortune* 500 manufacturing organization that we were recently working with made a telling comment in a management development strategy meeting: "What we need are more managers who know how to get the right results in the right way if we are going to be able to hit these aggressive numbers and take care of our customers and people." Although his organization was very successful financially, it was experiencing increasing competition, eroding profit margins, shortened life cycles on technologies, and rapid turnover of its product line. It became clear to all in this organization that managers had to become more results oriented if their organization was to endure.

■ How to Get Results: What Managers Think

If this tenet is indeed true, it begets the most important question, one that every manager must think about and explore: *How do I go about getting better results in the ultra-competitive workplace of the twenty-first century?* To explore this issue in greater depth, we surveyed over 1,600 high-performance managers on what they believe are the keys to getting results and learned a host of important lessons. Our sample of managers averaged forty-six years of age with seventeen years of management experience; 64 percent were men and 36 percent women. Participants in this study were all labeled high-performers" by their organization and collectively possessed over twenty-seven thousand years of management experience. Follow-up interviews were conducted with an additional four hundred high-performance managers to solicit further input, examples, cases, and personal anecdotes and quotes that we share throughout this book.

We analyzed the data generated from both the survey and interviews and ranked the results factors in their order of importance to the managers in this study. Table 1.1 contains the top twenty management fundamentals that these managers deemed most important in their quest for results.

The information in Table 1.1 lets us dispel several myths. First, when managers are described as being results oriented, they are frequently viewed as being too task oriented, with little or no regard for people or the human side of organizations. On

Table 1.1. Key Research Findings for Getting Results

1. Use effective and dynamic communication practices.
2. Lead by example to demonstrate character and competence.
3. Establish and maintain a clear and meaningful vision and mission.
4. Provide motivation to create ownership and accountability for results.
5. Clarify performance expectations with all employees.
6. Foster teamwork and cooperation.
7. Develop clear and balanced performance goals and metrics.
8. Develop key working relationships.
9. Provide ongoing employee training and education.
10. Conduct appropriate and systematic planning activities.
11. Remove performance barriers quickly.
12. Keep yourself current and practice personal development.
13. Provide ongoing performance feedback and coaching.
14. Demonstrate extreme care in staffing your operation.
15. Clarify your value-added role as manager.
16. Provide ongoing performance monitoring and measurement.
17. Equip people with resources they need to perform.
18. Proactively improve your processes.
19. Practice constructive employee appraisal and development.
20. Maintain balance in both your professional and personal life.

Note: n = 2,000+ managers.

the contrary, these findings make it clear that getting results requires a balance between effective people-oriented practices and effective task-oriented practices, with the balance favoring the people side of the equation. High-performance managers make this point loud and clear: unless you engage people power, you cannot create great long-term performance.[2]

Second, although the words of the legendary football coach Woody Hayes—"You win with people!"—ring true, concern for people alone does not bring a manager desired results. An executive friend of ours is often heard saying, "Even the best people can only get so far without effective systems, processes, support, and resources." This is a view shared by managers in this study: managers must be task oriented in very specific ways to create an overall process and workplace system that is set up to get desired results. Yet we know from previous research that many managers tend to gravitate toward task-oriented practices at the expense of people-oriented issues and that people-oriented issues are frequently lost or tossed aside in the heat of battle.[3] Thus, although most managers truly want better performance and the results that follow, they frequently lack the focus, skills, passion, knowledge, and balance necessary to create an effective personal management system that addresses both the people issues and the systems issues in concert.

■ The Rules of the Game: Five Absolutes for Getting Results

The ability of managers to get results and improve their performance is driven to a great extent by their ability to address what we have come to call the Five Absolutes for Getting Results. "There are no absolutes anymore" is a well-worn axiom of modern business—but it's simply not true. The intent of this oft-repeated saying is probably to remind us that the rules of business and the marketplace are constantly in a state of change (so don't look for pat answers or standardized solutions to fix complex problems or deficiencies). Yet this line of thinking can lead managers to look for a quick fix or ignore tried-and-true practices that can help make the complex issue of improving performance much easier to understand and address.

Based on our findings, it is our position that when it comes to getting results, there are a few critical results-oriented practices. We have carefully selected the word *absolute* as a moniker for each set of results-oriented practices that emerged from this research. An *absolute* is defined as something that possesses the characteristic of being complete in nature. We found that the twenty results-oriented practices identified by the managers in this study can be categorized into Five Absolutes for high performance.

Further, for a manager to create and sustain a level of complete performance that will produce desired results in these pressure-packed times, all of the following Five Absolutes must be present:

- *Absolute 1. Get everyone on the same page: Focus on the purpose of your organization.* Create and maintain a clear and unambiguous focus on desired results for yourself, your people, and your operation as a whole—and create a means to measure performance.
- *Absolute 2. Prepare for battle: Equip your operation with tools, talent, and technology.* Progressively staff your operation with high-quality people, develop effective planning practices, provide ongoing training and education for your people, and ensure people have the tools they need to get the job done.
- *Absolute 3. Stoke the fire of performance: Create a climate for results.* Create an operational climate that measures performance, provides ongoing performance measurement and feedback, motivates people, and removes barriers to performance in an ongoing and systematic fashion.
- *Absolute 4. Build bridges on the road to results: Nurture relationships with people.* Identify, foster, nurture, and sustain relationships, practice effective communication, and foster cooperation through the practice of trustworthy leadership with the people you need to get results.
- *Absolute 5. Keep the piano in tune: Practice continuous renewal.* Continuously improve and renew yourself, your processes, and your people, and maintain balance in all facets of your life for long-term success.

Together, these Five Absolutes represent the pieces of a puzzle, all of which managers must put together to create a complete high-performance system that is capable of getting and sustaining results. If one of the pieces of the puzzle is missing (or any piece is only partially in place), the performance puzzle is incomplete and performance will suffer. All the pieces must be brought together in unison, and dynamic and trustworthy leadership that creates real change and desired results must be provided by the manager. Figure 1.1 illustrates this concept, showing how each of the Five Absolutes represents a critical component that is needed to improve performance and get better results.

If a manager lacks skill in (or ignores) a particular area, results will not be optimal. In this context, it is easy to see why getting better results can be a daunting challenge—because it requires focus, skill, discipline, and passion in a host of different or even competing arenas. But herein is also the reason for hope, enthusiasm, and encouragement. Almost all managers have specific areas of performance that already work well, and others that can be identified, targeted, and improved upon to increase overall effectiveness.

■ Mastering the Five Managerial Absolutes

To identify areas of your performance that are currently effective and areas that need work to make you a more complete and effective manager, stop right now and complete the Getting Results Assessment in Worksheet 1.1. We return to this assessment in the last chapter to help you develop an improvement plan using what you learned from reading this book.

So what is it that you need to be working on to complete your performance puzzle? Do you have a clear sense of purpose for your operation? Do you have a meaningful set of goals and metrics that you and your people are pursuing? Are all of your people clearly focused on performing the duties that are most critical to the success of your operation? Do people in your operation cooperate with each other in serving your internal and external customers? Is effective staffing and training of personnel

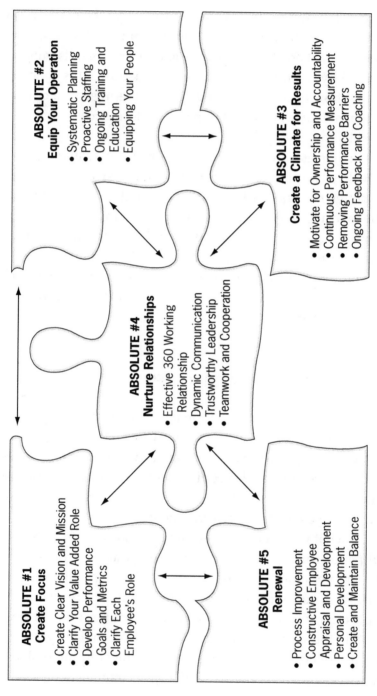

ABSOLUTE #1
Create Focus

- Create Clear Vision and Mission
- Clarify Your Value Added Role
- Develop Performance Goals and Metrics
- Clarify Each Employee's Role

ABSOLUTE #2
Equip Your Operation

- Systematic Planning
- Proactive Staffing
- Ongoing Training and Education
- Equipping Your People

ABSOLUTE #3
Create a Climate for Results

- Motivate for Ownership and Accountability
- Continuous Performance Measurement
- Removing Performance Barriers
- Ongoing Feedback and Coaching

ABSOLUTE #4
Nurture Relationships

- Effective 360 Working Relationship
- Dynamic Communication
- Trustworthy Leadership
- Teamwork and Cooperation

ABSOLUTE #5
Renewal

- Process Improvement
- Constructive Employee Appraisal and Development
- Personal Development
- Create and Maintain Balance

Figure 1.1. The Five Absolutes for Getting Results

■ **Worksheet 1.1.** ■
Getting Results Assessment

Instructions: Answer each of the following questions in an honest and open fashion to assess the extent to which you are effectively engaged in the practices that lead to improving performance and results. Use the following rating scale:

1=Never   2=Rarely   3=Sometimes   4=To a Great Extent   5=Always

To What Extent Do I . . .

1. Practice effective communications to understand others and to be understood?   _____

2. Lead by example and demonstrate competency and character in the workplace?   _____

3. Have a clear vision and mission for where I am leading my people?   _____

4. Hold people accountable and motivate them to increase their performance?   _____

5. Clarify performance expectations with all my employees?   _____

6. Foster cooperation and teamwork with the people who need each other to get results?   _____

7. Use clearly defined and balanced performance metrics to measure performance?   _____

8. Work at continually developing and nurturing key working relationships?   _____

9. Ensure that my people are properly trained and educated to get results?   _____

10. Employ appropriate and systematic planning practices?   _____

11. Work to rapidly remove performance barriers that get in the way of getting results?   _____

■ Worksheet 1.1. ■
Getting Results Assessment, Cont'd

---

12. Keep myself up-to-date with the skills necessary to be effective in my job? _____

13. Provide ongoing performance feedback and coaching to my people? _____

14. Take extreme care in staffing the operation? _____

15. Proactively clarify my value-added organizational role? _____

16. Regularly monitor and measure the operation's performance? _____

17. Work to make sure that people are properly equipped to perform their jobs? _____

18. Have mechanisms in place to improve processes on an ongoing basis? _____

19. Constructively appraise my employees' performance and establish plans for their development? _____

20. Work to maintain balance in all facets of my life? _____

Interpretation: Any practice that receives less than a score of 4 is a potential target behavior for improving your personal performance and propensity for getting better results.

a priority? Do you move to remove performance barriers in a timely fashion? Do you have a plan to improve your personal performance? Is developing your people an activity that you take seriously?

These are just a few of the critical questions that we will address in the rest of this book as we lay the foundation for developing a system for improving your ability to get results and your long-term career survival and success. In the end, your ability to improve your performance and corresponding results will be dictated to the greatest extent by your ability to develop and master the Five Absolutes that we are about to explore.

In these dynamic and competitive times, it is easy for managers to feel overwhelmed and perhaps even to begin to despair, because the organizational demands for improvement are never ending. Modern managers are being paid to get results for their organizations and their approach to leading people and creating effective business processes is critical in any effort to improve performance. But it is our purpose here to provide all our readers with a sense of hope and optimism about their future. Our core belief is a simple one: as things get more complex, complicated, dynamic, and fast-paced, managers at all levels must get back to mastering the managerial absolutes that drive improvement, because it is here that the seeds of success or failure are found.

CHAPTER SUMMARY

As organizations move into the ultra-competitive twenty-first century, they are becoming more performance oriented and performance sensitive. Research on organizational downsizing practices points to the fact that what managers do and how well they do it is critical to their career survival. Our research on career success points to the fact that conceptual, interpersonal, and technical skills are all very important. And being able to make good decisions, handle stress, build a broad base of work experience, and acquire a mentor are key as well. But the single most important factor for keeping your job and getting ahead is to build an excellent performance record based on your ability to get results. The research shared in this book will show you how to go about improving your performance by focusing your energies and developing effective management practices that we have come to call the "Five Absolutes" for achieving high performance. Perfecting these management fundamentals will play a critical role in your future, which you can greatly influence by your actions and what you do with the information in this book. Without this foundation of fundamentals it is very difficult to build a track record and career of high performance.

Absolute #1

Get Everyone on the Same Page: Focus on the Purpose of Your Organization

After the Chicago Bulls "three-peated" for the NBA title in 1996, Michael Jordan made a simple yet profound statement: "We set our eyes on the title, we knew what we had to do to get things done, and we just took care of business!" Jordan's comment demonstrates one of the most awesome attributes of elite performers: their uncanny ability to focus on a desired goal and to pursue that goal with both process and passion. We see this highly developed sense of focus and concentration quite clearly in athletes. But we know that is also true of all successful performers, whether they are scientists, inventors, architects, entrepreneurs, writers, computer gurus, artists, engineers, or managers. The practices described by Michael Jordan are all paramount to leading any organization forward. One easy way to think of this process of focus is found in the phrase "getting everyone on the same page." In this chapter, you learn the four practices for creating focus in your organization, no matter what your level of management. But why should you bother to do this?

■ The Need for Purpose and Direction

Most people long for a clear sense of purpose and direction in all facets of their lives. Without purpose and direction, people feel frustration, confusion, alienation, and eventually withdrawal. When a clear sense of purpose and direction is present, people feel focused. In a focused organization, members can make sense out of the myriad of activities and see all as movement in one identifiable direction. Creating focus creates an "organizational glue" that binds people and activities together. To illustrate this point in the workplace, consider what happens to an operation that has become unfocused.

When an Enterprise Is Unfocused

Imagine that you have just been promoted into a new position in your organization to head up a large customer service department. It becomes apparent after several days on the job that the department has no sense of direction whatsoever. Customers are an enigma and tend to complain a lot, things seem very disorganized, employees pretty much do what they've always done—they don't get along with each other and indulge in a lot of finger-pointing. You can't tell who's right, if anybody is, as you have only a few rather broad performance measures, none of which look particularly good at the moment. When you took this new position, the only real input you got from your boss was the mandate, "clean up this mess." When you stopped and talked to a group of employees on their break your first day you asked, "Well, how are things going?" Their collective response was, "Why don't you tell us!" And two of your younger supervisors approached you twice the same day and asked, "So where are we going?" As a result, three questions keep running through your mind: "Why did I ever take this job?" "How did this department get to this point?" and "Where do I start?"

Without a clear sense of direction, clearly defined goals, and clearly defined roles, any work unit—whether group, team, department, division, or organization—can find itself engaged in a great deal of action without meaningful outcomes. Which is exactly what an organization cannot afford to do in today's extremely competitive global marketplace!

■ Four Critical Practices for Creating Focus

In our research, results-oriented managers identified four specific practices that all managers need to create appropriate focus and direction for their people (Figure 2.1).

1. Get everyone in your operation on the same page in terms of the building overriding purpose and mission of the work unit. In modern enterprises, everyone should know what the organization needs and how each job contributes to the overall success.
2. Clarify your own value-added role in the operation. You do this by getting input from superiors, subordinates, and anyone else who can make your job more meaningful in supporting results-oriented activity.
3. Help your work unit develop clear and meaningful goals and measures so that performance can be tracked against a useful scorecard.

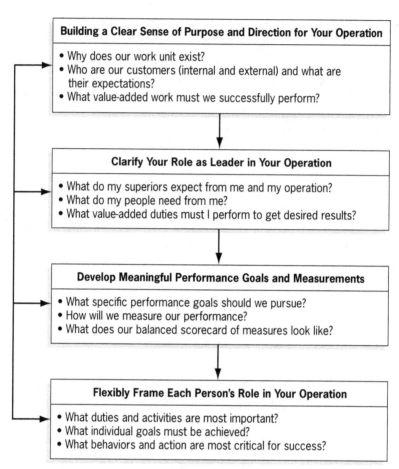

Figure 2.1. The Four Critical Practices:
Getting Everyone on the Same Page by Creating Focus

4. Flexibly frame each person's role in your operation in order
    to help create a clear, unambiguous picture of what *every* em-
    ployee must do to help the operation achieve its overarch-
    ing mission and goals (results).

    Your proficiency in these specific areas will go a long way
toward addressing the oft-heard organizational complaint, "Does
anybody around here have a clue of where we are going and
what we are doing?" Without leadership on these key issues, the
art of getting results becomes difficult if not impossible.

■ **Practice 1:**
Create a Clear Sense of Purpose for Your Operation

IRREFUTABLE PERFORMANCE PRINCIPLE: Work units with a clear sense of purpose outperform those that do not have a clearly defined mission.

A great deal has been written about the necessity of creating a clear mission for an organization as a whole and about the benefits that derive from such a process.[1] Yet there is surprisingly little discussion in many circles for taking the same critical thinking process and applying it to *all work units* within that organization. An organization's global mission to be "a world-class producer of high technology components through cutting-edge product development and customer partnering" can go a long way to help define an organization's purpose, but still provide little sense of direction to a department of customer service personnel or to a maintenance crew.

At the organizational level, we know that market leaders are successful when they clearly define their mission in terms of achieving one of three things: low cost, great products, or superior customer service.[2] Market leaders select one primary mission as a means to compete, and then provide acceptable levels of performance in the other two areas. Their lesson is a simple one: Success results from focusing clearly on a specific mission and creating an organization to fulfill that mission.

Today, managers at all levels are frequently being encouraged to run their operations as if they were their own businesses. To support this, they are being empowered to take care of their customers, control their costs, and improve their processes. Managers are being encouraged to think like owners, and owners tend to be very focused on doing the right things and not wasting a lot of time or money (and not doing stupid things that do not enhance performance—because it is their money). From this perspective, the first and most critical job of results-oriented managers is to help their operations develop a clear focus. You, as manager, are responsible for creating a clear sense of purpose for your operations, regardless of the level or function. This purpose can be used to create an overarching sense of "this is who we are and what we do."

A good starting point for a manager is to get all of the people in your operation on the same page by identifying the overriding purpose and mission of the work unit. In modern enterprises, everyone should be able to see the big picture and understand why the unit exists and what actions are most important for the operation to be successful. And while many people toil over the definitions of the words *purpose, vision,* and *mission,* we find most effective leaders using these words interchangeably with the intent of creating and describing direction for their operations.

If the people that work with you and for you have no clear sense of their purpose in the organization or in what direction they should be moving, the reason is one of two things—and both of them are unacceptable. Either you have not created a clear sense of purpose and direction for your people, or you have been ineffective in communicating it to your people.

Here's an exercise to answer the question: *Do your people have a clear and accurate sense of the purpose of your operation and what needs to be done to be successful?*

Find Out Now—Do We Have a Clear Mission?

1. Give a business card to one of your key people and say, "On the back of the card, write out a mission statement that captures the purpose, goals, and reason that your work unit exists." (Use a business card to force them to be concise.)
2. Repeat the process at least five times with different stakeholders and see what you learn.

Most managers find there is a significant difference of opinion as to what the work unit is really trying to achieve.

You will use your mission statement to drive the specific activities that your unit pursues, as well as use it to determine what work your unit will not pursue. Behind the entire process, you will be looking for answers, with help, to the following questions:

- Why does our work unit exist?
- Who are our customers and what are their needs and expectations?
- What value-added work must be successfully performed?

The answers to each of these questions are critical to getting your people and operation properly focused on the big picture, one that is easily lost in the day-to-day heat of battle. Throughout the steps that follow, you will see these questions used in some form.

The Mission Statement

Here are five steps for creating a mission statement. This important task involves—besides the writing itself—meeting with your manager, key members of your group, and finally your entire group.

1. *Meet with your manager.*

Meet with your superior to get a good sense of what that person needs from your work unit as a whole. You need input on three specific questions to begin the process of creating a clear sense of purpose for your group.

- What specific outcomes do you expect from this work unit?
- Who are the unit's customers and what are their expectations?
- What value-added work must the unit successfully perform?

Be sure to provide your input to the discussion to create a shared sense of agreement and alignment between the two parties. The manager can then create an initial draft of the group's mission statement to take back to the work unit and share with the staff.

2. *Write the initial draft.*

Write an initial draft of your proposed mission statement. Your mission statement must address the key questions in these terms:

- What is our business?
- Who are our customers?
- What are our priorities?
- What activities are most critical to our success?

Remember that effective mission statements create an overarching sense of purpose for the work unit's activities and should meet the following criteria:

They are simple and to the point.
They serve as a criterion to guide future actions.
They provide clear direction that allows the work unit to identify factors for measurement.
They define what the work unit could and should stand for.

3. *Have your key staff review the proposed statement.*

In a meeting or retreat setting, ask your key staff to review and refine the mission statement. In this way, you encourage ownership and understanding of what the work unit is all about and what everyone is trying to achieve. Discussion might proceed in any or all of the following directions, all of which are OK:

- Why are we having this discussion and is this a waste of time?
- Is this really what our work unit is trying to achieve?
- Is the statement realistic and meaningful?
- Can it be used as a test to determine what value these activities add?

Using a facilitator in this process can be a real benefit to move the discussion along and encourage meaningful dialogue.

4. *Circulate the statement among your staff.*

When a refined version of the mission statement has been developed, circulate it among your whole staff. Describe where the mission came from and what you intend to do with it. Give people an opportunity to meet in small groups and review the mission—by reading the statement, clarifying it in response to any questions that arise, and offering any additional inputs to help get everybody on the same page.

5. *Review the responses, then draft and circulate the final mission statement.*

Next, you or your key personnel review the groups' responses, using them to refine the work unit's mission statement. Draft a clear, concise mission statement, and be sure to circulate it to all members of the work unit so people can begin to think about how to better achieve your mission in word and deed.

Practical Example—Mission Statements That Work

A newly formed operations center in a Fortune 500 organization was struggling to define what it was ultimately trying to achieve as a business unit. After several drafts from the leaders and the input of all seventy-plus members of the operation, the group took a sixty-word statement of purpose down to these fifteen words:

> Our mission is to provide excellent and cost-effective portfolio management with superior customer service.

This statement defined the primary purpose (portfolio management), established the priorities (cost-effectiveness and customer service), and set a standard of performance (excellent and superior activity). This statement then became part of the operating culture not by the simple fact that it was hanging in frames on the walls of offices or printed on the back of business cards or repeated at regular department meetings but rather because it directly influenced planning activities, training, budgeting, daily decision making, and process improvement activities.

As another example, a production unit of a midsized automotive parts supplier crafted the following mission statement to create purpose for all their activities: Our department exists to produce high-quality parts, on time and in a cost-conscious manner, through effective planning, machine utilization, and team ownership of the production process. As in the first example, this mission statement clarified the department's primary purpose (high-quality parts), established the priorities (timeliness and cost-consciousness), and stated the key activities (planning, machine usage, and team ownership).

Although a piece of paper with a mission clearly stated cannot by itself create meaningful purpose for a work unit, the process of developing it and its use thereafter clearly can. And even then, your work isn't finished. Once your mission is defined, it must become part of the cultural fabric of your operation. It must be used and aligned again and again to create and maintain clear direction—direction that is based on current operational demands and customer needs. Results-oriented managers in this research were unambiguous and passionate in their opinion that improving performances starts with a clearly defined mission that everyone knows and understands.

■ Practice 2: Clarify Your Role as Leader in the Operation

IRREFUTABLE PERFORMANCE PRINCIPLE: Managers improve their performance and the performance of their people when they perform value-added practices and minimize non–value-added activity.

These days, when you ask managers what duties they perform, the flippant response is frequently, "It might be easier to tell you the few things I'm not responsible for!" or "How much time do you have?" Many gains in white-collar productivity have come from downsizing the managerial ranks and simply asking (ordering) managers to do more with less.[3] While most everyone is indeed busier than in the past, this does not necessarily translate into improved performance and better results. Therefore, it becomes important that you determine how well you are measuring up to the standard of performing value-added work in your role as a manager.

Here's an exercise to answer the question: *Am I performing the value-added functions that are most critical to my operation's performance and success?* This exercise can be approached by working through your own manager and by approaching your own work unit. For best results, do both.

Find Out Now—Are You Doing What Really Needs to Be Done?

1. Stop and reflect on what duties you typically perform in your current job as a manager.

2. Now make a list of all the specific things that you do and don't worry about prioritizing them.

3. Ask your superior in the organization to make a list of the duties that you should be performing (say you are being proactive in aligning yourself with the current needs of the operation). Once you have both lists, lay them down side by side and see how much overlap exists.

4. To approach the same issue from a different perspective, identify a group of key personnel in your work unit and ask them this simple question: "What do you need from me to help you get your work done and take care of our customers?" Have people answer the question individually, and then discuss their lists collectively, making a master list of what people need from you as their manager.

5. Compare the three lists and see what can be learned about how you view your job compared with your boss and your people.

The purpose of this exercise was to focus on the importance of aligning your daily activities with the demands and needs of your operations. It goes without saying that most people in managerial positions are very, very busy. But the question arises, busy doing what? As a manager you need to draw on three important sources of information to review, analyze, and solidify the role you should play in your operation's performance. Remember the old saying, "If there is a mist on the pulpit, there is probably a fog in the pews." So if you are not perfectly clear about what you need to do to successfully lead your people, you are not in a position to help maximize their performance.

Get Aligned with the Needs of Your Boss

As a manager, you have to meet the needs and expectations of your superiors while at the same time performing critical functions for your direct reports who need you (to various degrees) to get their work done. In study after study, we have found that there is frequently a significant gap between what a superior thinks a manager's job really entails and what the manager thinks that job entails. This gap frequently manifests itself in the form of tension and discomfort around such practices as formal performance reviews, pay-for-performance payouts, promotion discussions, and developmental reviews. On these occasions, both parties can have a hard time agreeing on what basis to evaluate past performance and on what specific performance improvements are needed. Managers interested in improving their performance need to start by being proactive in aligning themselves with their boss's performance expectations (especially since many superiors will not take the initiative). A savvy manager will come to consensus with the manager at the next higher level on the following issues and will stay aligned throughout the year by meeting regularly with the superior to talk about performance issues and improvements:

- What specific results do you expect from my work unit?
- What measurables will be used to assess performance?
- What do you see as the most important duties and tasks that we need to perform in this job based on your previous experience?

The answers to these questions are critical to making sure that, as a subordinate, you are in a good position to meet the real needs of your superior. Your boss is more likely to get behind your efforts at improving the performance of your work unit when your support and actions are properly aligned with what the boss needs.

Get Aligned with the Needs of Your People

The second part of clarifying your role is getting aligned with the needs of your people. Having your people collectively tell you the specifics of what they need from you to get their work done allows you the opportunity to improve their performance by value-added activity on your part. Once you know what your people need, you must take action to best support their performance.

The Performance Script

If you don't already have a list of what your people want and need from you, make one now. This list, called a *performance script*, identifies what needs to be done, for whom, and when. Step 4 of the exercise headed "Are You Doing What Really Needs to Be Done?" can provide you with data needed to craft an effective performance script. By using and enacting this script you will best help your people excel.

Practical Example—
Using a Performance Script to Get Leaders to Lead

A high-tech computer assembly plant traditionally had a job description for its front-line managers that had been developed by the organization's managers and HR specialists. Industry competition was squeezing profit margins and top management became increasingly concerned with controlling costs. An effort was made to get employees to develop performance scripts of the key activities that managers needed to perform to facilitate the ever-changing work of the employees. Based on the input of the workforce as well as their superiors, the role of the front-line manager evolved from being one of a "strong-armed baby-sitter" to that of a planner, coach, and expediter. The workers told management what they needed to get better results, and management, if they really wanted better performance, had to put up or shut up. The workforce needed the following key actions from their front-line managers to improve performance. This became their performance script.

- Do effective pre-shift work and inventory scheduling on all production lines.
- Meet daily with maintenance teams to ensure that both immediate and preventive maintenance concerns are properly prioritized, addressed, and followed up on.
- Assure proper staffing levels for each work unit during each and every shift.
- Make sure that all new and temporary workers are properly trained to perform their jobs.
- Conduct informative pre-shift meetings to establish clear shift goals on all critical measures and ensure that all employees know what to expect during the shift.
- Monitor all key performance metrics during the shift and conduct a mid-shift meeting to communicate performance and address and resolve any problems with the shift.
- Provide both individual and work unit feedback and coaching to help improve performance on each and every shift.
- Conduct a post-shift review with the relief manager to communicate status, set performance goals, and anticipate any problems for the following shift.

We have seen this process work in many organizations as long as managers are simply willing to ask their people (including peers and customers as well) how they might best serve them. Asking requires keeping one's ego in check and being willing to listen and change daily behavior. At this facility managers became very proficient at facilitating the work of their employees through this alignment process.

Define Your Value-Added Action and Just Do It
The ultimate decision of what constitutes value-added behavior on the part of a leader falls squarely on the shoulders of each and every manager. You have to reconcile the demands of your boss and the needs of your employees in deciding how and what you do in your job. You create a more value-added role for yourself by aligning yourself effectively with these two partners. The third critical source of information in establishing your role in the operation is yourself—your own past experience and understanding of the situation.

Once that role has been determined, you also need to remove non–value-added activity that detracts from your ability to perform key functions. Sitting in endless meetings, ploughing through mountains of e-mail, generating reports that are not meaningful, taking useless phone calls and engaging in other non–value-added activities can prevent a manager from performing the functions that are truly going to improve performance. The key point is this: results-oriented managers do not waste time.

Using Worksheet 2.1 or a blank sheet of paper, list value-added activities that must increase, based on the input you've gotten from your boss and people. At the same time, list the non–value-added activities that are eating up the time you need for more critical activities, those that provide value to your employees and customers.

Once you have identified what activities are most important to your performance, describe the characteristics of superior performance in each area. It is not good enough to know what

■ Worksheet 2.1. Allocation of Attention ■			
The Value-Added Performance Activities in My Job That Must Increase		The Non–Value-Added Activities That Must Decrease	
Activity	Standard of performance	Activity	Preventive action

you must do; you must describe how to do it effectively and develop a commitment to specific standards of performance. Proactive managers will ask their superiors to make this list of activities and performance standards part of the manager's regular performance review so as to create accountability for change. At the same time, managers must monitor their personal performance to stay focused on the right activities and to minimize non–value-added activities that can easily derail or destroy a manager's ability to do more of the right kinds of things.

■ **Practice 3:**
Develop Meaningful Performance Goals and Measures

IRREFUTABLE PERFORMANCE PRINCIPLE: Work units that have clearly defined performance goals and effective performance measures will outperform those that do not, all things being equal.

Now that your unit is focused and you've written your performance script, you need to be able to measure performance and direct activities. The question is generally not *whether* to set goals, but rather which goals are most appropriate, how they should be established, and how to measure performance. The answer to each of these questions is critical to improving performance. Put most simply, goal-setting and measurement support the age-old adage, "It's tough to manage what you don't measure!"

Here's an exercise to answer the question: *Does my operation pursue and measure meaningful and balanced performance goals on an ongoing basis that focus on desired results?* Consider how well your unit is doing right now, and check the appropriate boxes in Worksheet 2.2. Once you've completed the worksheet, answer the following questions:

Find Out Now—Are You Monitoring Your Measures?

1. How confident are you of the accuracy of each of these measures?
2. If your boss completed the same assessment, how much overlap would there be in the ratings of performance?
3. If your people completed the same assessment, how much overlap would there be in their ratings with yours?

Results-oriented managers are typically very focused on achieving desired outcomes. That is to say they tend to be goal oriented. The use of goal setting as a management practice is as old as the pharaoh's setting production goals for the number of bricks made by the slaves in ancient Egypt (see Exodus 5). For the past fifty years, management by objectives (MBO) has been a widespread organizational practice, employing goal setting as a motivational and control device.[4] Goal setting and MBO practices were widely used among the managers in this study. But are goals alone enough? The managers in this study provided a warning to us that traditional goal setting and MBO can easily

■ **Worksheet 2.2. Performance Snapshot** ■

Performance Measures	Performance Rating						
	Don't Know	Poor	Less Than Satisfactory	Satisfactory	Very Good	Excellent
Customer Satisfaction	☐	☐	☐	☐	☐	☐
Operating Efficiency	☐	☐	☐	☐	☐	☐
Financial Performance	☐	☐	☐	☐	☐	☐
Quality of Product or Service	☐	☐	☐	☐	☐	☐
Employee Performance	☐	☐	☐	☐	☐	☐
Process Improvement	☐	☐	☐	☐	☐	☐

focus exclusively on specific financial or outcome-based measures without taking into consideration more balanced goals and outcomes and the processes used to achieve them.

The quality movement of the past twenty years has demonstrated the importance of developing goals and performance targets that go well beyond simply measuring financial and production-based objectives. This emphasis has been underscored by the evolution of the reengineering movement of the past decade, with the focus expanding to include a host of process measures that involve operational performance. Most recently, the "balanced scorecard" movement heralded by Kaplan and Norton has emerged as a process whose aim is to present management with a concise summary of the key success factors of a business and to facilitate the alignment of business operations with overall strategy.[5] This process provides a medium to translate vision into a clear set of performance objectives. These objectives are then translated into a system of effective measurements that create strategic focus for the entire organization.

Given this background there is a very good chance that your organization is employing some goal-setting practices of its own at present. Nonetheless, we would like to offer some advice that might enhance your effectiveness in this critical area based on the input of the managers in this study. Managers frequently set goals and objectives without looking at why they are doing so and at what cost. Although summary financial measures are indeed important they do not provide a complete picture. Another old adage hits home here: "You get what you measure, so you'd better measure the right things."

Our advice to each and every manager we work with is simple: To create focus on balanced results, you need to clarify your goals and measurements in four key areas. Measurement always starts with the goals you are pursuing, and the concept of balance is critical here. Therefore ask yourself these key questions to help determine the goals to pursue:

- What goals will tell us if we are on track in serving our organizational mission and operational needs, and how will we measure performance?
- What goals will tell us if we are effectively serving our customers, and how will we measure performance?
- What goals will tell us if we are improving our employees' performance, and how will we measure our performance?
- What goals will tell us if we are performing effectively financially?

Create a Balanced Scorecard

The answers to these questions should allow you to develop a *performance scorecard* for your work unit that helps you to clearly communicate to all your people what is important to your unit's performance. Creating an effective set of performance goals and measures takes time and effort. So if there is to be a value-added process, it must be well conceived, properly focused and implemented, well communicated, and used with care to create meaningful focus.

Goals should possess criteria that are SMART: Specific, Measurable, Attainable, Results-oriented, and Time-sensitive. Based on the input of the high-performing manager in our study, six primary performance goals and measurements were identified as being critical for developing a balanced scorecard that creates proper focus for balanced results. These goals and measurements include the following:

- *Customer Goals and Measures:* sales growth, customer satisfaction, repeat business, growth in order size, customer referrals, and market expansion.

- *Operating Efficiency Goals and Measures:* productivity, equipment utilization, cycle time measures, machine downtime, waste and scrap, operating cost structures, and developmental costs.
- *Financial Performance Goals and Measures:* revenues, gross profits, net profits, operating margins, budget variances, cash flow, return on investment, and net return on equity.
- *Quality Goals and Measures:* defects, reject rates, cost to correct quality mistakes, and conformance and nonconformance to quality standards.
- *Employee Performance Goals and Measures:* turnover, absenteeism, safety, individual/team productivity, employee satisfaction, training, and workplace grievances.
- *Process Improvement Goals and Measures:* reduced cycle time, simplified work procedures, improved performance tracking metrics and systems, and more effective corrective action activity.

Now each of these key performance areas must be translated into specific goals and measures that give you the balanced focus that everyone agrees is critical to your organization's success. By balance we mean measures that provide a picture of the *complete* performance issues that are necessary for success. A short-term and long-term perspective is critical to this discussion as well so that, as a results-oriented leader, you can keep a dual focus on the short-term and the long-term time horizons. It is equally important that your employees and superiors agree on both the dimensions on the scorecard and agree on how and when these dimensions will be measured. Communication is critical here as your family of measures must be understood by everyone. Effective leaders take great care in creating balanced goals and measures and making sure that everyone understands how performance is being measured and what specific metrics are critical to success. Worksheet 2.3 will help you to create effective goals and measure for your organization.

■ Worksheet 2.3. Measurement Families ■				
	Short-Term		Long-Term	
Family of Measures	Goals	Measures	Goals	Measures
Customer-focused performance				
Operating efficiency				
Financial performance				
Quality				
Employee performance				
Process performance				

As a results-oriented leader, you will be able to make the following statements confidently both to your superior and to your employees as a litmus test of your effectiveness in creating goals that get everyone on the same page:

- We are in agreement on our goals and measures.
- We are confident in the accuracy of the measurement data.
- Our goals and measures are properly balanced.
- We are looking at both the short-term and long-term horizons.

Based on the input of the managers in this study, we conclude that extreme care and energy must be devoted to creating effective goals and measurements that support your mission. Once these metrics are in place it is imperative that you use them and the accurate data they provide as input for guiding your operation and your people. Data-based decision making can prevent you from being in the dark about how your operation is truly performing. Or (to update an old adage), "In God we trust, all others bring data."

Practical Example—How Are Things Really Going?

Bill's boss asked him to stop by and see him at the end of the day. After a brief social exchange, the boss asked Bill a question that caught him a little off guard. "How are things going in your department?" Bill's nervous reaction was typical, given the question: "Things are OK. Why? Is there a problem?" "No, Bill, there isn't a problem that I am aware of, but do you really know how well your department is performing?" the boss asked a second time. Bill's response was, "I think so and I think we are doing fine," to which his boss said, "That is not going to be good enough anymore." Then the boss went on to explain that since the recent merger the new parent organization was requiring managers at all levels to create effective measurements in a variety of critical areas. In the past Bill had been held accountable for budget utilization and several efficiency measures on an annual basis. Now Bill was being asked to develop and maintain specific performance goals and measures in a host of areas that more accurately reflected ongoing performance. He was initially discouraged at this new corporate mandate, but his boss said, "Bill, I know this sounds like more work than it might be worth but the more I think about it, the more it makes good business sense to set up a variety of balanced goals and measures that can help get all of us pulling in the same direction and measuring the right things. We need to develop a more useful measurement system so we can take more appropriate action to run our operation. Let's talk about how you can answer the question, 'How are things going in your department?' using some measures that will help you better lead your operation." Although Bill was not fired up by the prospect of doing this he knew that his boss was right and appreciated his willingness to help him develop a better scorecard of performance. The process of turning this apparent negative into a positive had begun, and Bill now knew that he would need more than just his feelings on any given day to know how his operation was really performing.

■ **Practice 4: Frame Each Person's Role in Your Operation**

IRREFUTABLE PERFORMANCE PRINCIPLE: Without effective leadership employees find it difficult at best to keep their activity aligned with the current needs of an operation.

Things become more clearly focused for your employees as you clarify the purpose of your work unit, develop a better sense of your value-added role, and create clear goals and performance measurements for your operation. But the most critical step still remains: to help each and every person in your operation clearly define their value-added role in getting results. We call this form of help flexibly framing a person's role—*flexibly*, because as organizations change, individual employee responsibilities need to change to keep up with changing operational needs; *framing*, because everyone needs to have a reasonably clear sense of where their duties, goals, and authority stop and start. Although it might be popular to suggest tearing up job descriptions and making claims like "we are all responsible for doing whatever it takes to get things done around here," our research continues to show that results-oriented leaders help their people create value-added roles for themselves that are unambiguous and clearly focused on an ongoing basis. Stated quite simply: people do want and need to know what their jobs really entail.

Why Effective Delegation Is So Important

In Douglas McGregor's seminal work, *The Human Side of Enterprise* (1960), effective delegation was described as one of the four most important management practices necessary to optimize human performance in the workplace.[6] Why? Delegation clarified the employee's role in getting things done. And while the term *delegation* is often used interchangeably with such terms as *empowerment, performance planning,* and *role clarification,* the process is best described as *the act of distributing and entrusting work to the people in your charge and granting them the authority they need to get the work done.* The goal of a results-oriented leader is to give the right work to the right people at the right time, and with the right resources and authority—a task that in a rapidly changing environment like ours is often quite challenging. Yet with fewer resources and more downsizing, companies can ill-afford to have employees not clearly focused on getting desired results. When you as a manager must get results with and through people, and those people do not clearly know their role in the operation, this process becomes bankrupt.

Here's an exercise to answer the question: *Do your people have a clear and accurate picture of what their job really entails and the authority they need to get results?*

Find Out Now—Are You and Your People Aligned?

1. Pick out your best employee and ask them to make a list of the duties they perform and the goals they are currently pursuing. Ask them to prioritize their list as well.
2. Describe the employee's job yourself, before you look at the list.
3. Now compare your lists. How much overlap exists?
4. Repeat the process with one of your employees whose performance is not where it needs to be. Are you and your people on the same page in terms of what needs to be done to get results?

People are generally most productive and efficient when they have a very clear idea of what is expected of them. Yet in organizational settings it is common to hear statements like "I'm never really quite sure what my boss thinks my job is," or "I'm not sure who is responsible for that," or "It sure is tough to get things done without the authority I need," or "I wonder what I am going to be held accountable for at appraisal time." All these comments strongly suggest that the process of delegation is not being practiced effectively. Otherwise, employees would be clear on their role and the role of others in getting results. Quite simply, this happens because their job responsibilities have never been flexibly framed.

Delegation as Three Interrelated Activities

As a manager, you can improve your skills for getting employees properly focused and prepared to perform a value-added job for their operations. Delegation is a process that involves three distinct but highly interrelated activities:

- *Clarifying Responsibilities.* Creating an obligation to do work by clarifying subordinate duties, work assignments, and goals through effective communication.
- *Empowerment.* Ensuring the subordinate has the power, sanction, knowledge, information, and resources necessary to fulfill the assigned responsibilities.
- *Providing Accountability.* Developing ongoing control and feedback mechanisms to determine if work is being performed as desired. Performance planning and performance management skills are very necessary here.

This critical process cannot be viewed as a one-shot deal—it must be a set of ongoing activities. Delegation must be thought of as a triangle (like the one in Figure 2.2) in that each activity represents a vertex that if not present will cause the structure to crumble. This process is always based on effective communication, trust, and ongoing interaction. If the manager doing the delegating neglects any of these activities, problems will follow. As an example, if responsibilities are not clearly communicated and understood, the employee will feel confusion and uncertainty—and this uncertainty will have a negative impact on the

Figure 2.2. The Delegation Triangle

employee's effectiveness. If adequate empowerment has not taken place, the subordinate will become frustrated and feel hamstrung because of the lack of the decision-making clout, sanction, or resources needed to get the job done. Last, if accountability is not provided in terms of ongoing performance appraisal and feedback, the employee can feel unappreciated or, worse yet, can continue to do work that is substandard without feeling the need to change. For any manager trying to improve performance, whether in a high-tech Internet company or an organization providing an old-line service such as health care, these outcomes are the kiss of death.

Most managers are well aware of the problems associated with ineffective delegation and role ambiguity and can usually cite examples from their own experience of the problems that develop when any part of the process is neglected. It is at this point that we run into a phenomenon that we have come to call the "delegation dilemma": most managers do know how and why to delegate, but they fail to take the time to do so in a complete and ongoing fashion. Many have concluded that managers are ineffective delegators because they are reluctant to share power, don't trust their subordinates, or don't understand delegation—or they are just plain afraid to delegate. These perspectives can be used to explain select cases of poor delegation, but the analysis is incomplete. Failing to take the time and effort is often a bigger problem for many managers. Regardless of the cause, ineffective delegation is a results buster!

Practical Example—The Delegation Dilemma

Our position on the importance of the delegation dilemma is based on years of observing managers and supervisors struggling to become effective at clarifying their employees' roles even after mandates to do so and receiving delegation skills training. A common pattern of this struggle has emerged that is illustrated in the following story.

A large manufacturing organization had recently trained 105 managers in specific delegation skills (clarifying duties and goals, empowerment, ongoing performance appraisal, providing effective feedback) because of problems that emerged from an organizational needs assessment.[7] Upon completion of the intense training, managers stated that they felt they had a very thorough understanding of the process of delegation. Yet a survey of their employees one year later revealed that these same managers were not practicing delegation in a complete and ongoing fashion (despite their subordinates' belief that they generally had the ability to do so). Specifically, employees were still frustrated with the lack of clarity of job assignments, the inadequate authority granted, and the poor quality and quantity of performance feedback they received in a rapidly changing organization. This was in turn having a negative effect on employee performance.

Follow-up interviews with managers revealed an interesting commonality. As a group, they believed they made initial progress at improving their delegation skills by meeting with each of their subordinates to clear the air and discuss current job responsibilities and authority. However, once these initial meetings were held managers stated that they struggled with taking the time to meet with their subordinates on a regular basis to clarify changing job requirements, authority, and resource requirements and to conduct ongoing appraisals and provide feedback.

This dilemma has been observed over and over again as managers who know the right thing to do as delegators fail to take the time to do it. This results in limiting the effectiveness of their employees, wasting resources, and hurting the managers themselves in the long run.

Plan and Manage Your Employees' Performance

To maximize the performance of individual employees, focusing their energy and activity becomes quite important. To this end, results-oriented managers have great prowess in clarifying and communicating employee responsibilities, goals, and authority to their people.

Once this focus is established the manager must manage performance on an ongoing basis by:

1. Monitoring employees' performance on an ongoing basis
2. Providing ongoing performance feedback to reinforce desired behaviors and help remove undesirable behaviors and outcomes
3. Addressing and removing performance barriers when they occur

Performance management and coaching will be discussed in greater detail in Chapter Four.

These practices must be ongoing to keep the employees' roles aligned with the needs of customers and the operation. It is equally important to come to a shared sense of agreement concerning what the employees should *not* be doing in their job. Effective leaders help their people learn how to avoid wasting time and energy pursuing non–value-added activities.

Clarifying each employee's role and keeping the person aligned with operational demands is critical to improving operational performance and getting results. And since most jobs are rapidly changing and speed is more of a necessity than ever before, this process must be repeated in shorter cycles than even a decade ago. Without aligned and empowered people pursuing SMART goals in unity, your operation's performance will never reach its full potential.

CHAPTER SUMMARY

For managing at any level, focus is critical. Results-oriented managers create focus for their work unit, themselves, and their people. One way to ensure success is to follow four key practices that our studies have shown to be beneficial.

Successful managers must first get all of their employees on the same page in terms of the overriding purpose and mission of the work unit. The reason is that in modern enterprises everyone should be able to see the big picture and understand why the unit exists and what actions are most important for the operation to succeed. Second, successful managers clarify their own value-added roles in the operation, getting input from superiors, subordinates, and anyone else who can make the managers' job more results oriented. Third, successful managers help their work unit develop clear and meaningful goals and measures. In this way, performance can be tracked against a useful scorecard. Finally, successful managers help create a clear, unambiguous picture of what every employee must do on the job to help the operation achieve its overarching mission and goals.

A manager's proficiency in these specific areas will go a long way toward addressing the oft-heard organizational complaint, "Does anybody around here have a clue of where we are going and what we are doing?" Without focused leadership, the art of getting results becomes difficult if not impossible. In the words of one of the managers in our study, "If you are in charge of any group of people and you are trying to get things done, then you'd better get everybody singing the same song, or the music you make will be a funeral dirge."

Absolute #2

Prepare for Battle:
Equip Your Operation with
Tools, Talent, and Technology

Several years ago, before a college bowl game, we witnessed the pre-game activities of a very successful Division I college football coach and team. The locker room was quiet and quite orderly as people dressed for the game. Before taking to the field the team knelt, and after a minute of silence the head coach said, in a very businesslike fashion, "I don't have to tell you how important this game is to all of us. . . . Let's go out and do what we've been preparing to do since last summer!" The team took to the field and won the game 40–37 in the first college football overtime ever in a bowl game. After the game we asked the head coach why his pre-game speech wasn't more of a "motivating, fire-up kind of rah-rah thing." His response was noteworthy: "If we are not prepared in all ways to do battle, all the rah-rah in the world won't win the game. . . . It all goes back to preparation."

While nearly every manager has recently been reminded of the importance of being a coach, many people mistakenly believe that their primary, and even sole, responsibility as a coach is to provide feedback and encouragement to their players. While this dimension of coaching is important, it is only one part of a manager's role as a coach. The larger part deals directly with the issue of a coach's responsibility to prepare players to compete.

The managers in our research support this position, in that they find that certain preparation practices must be in place to equip an operation to achieve desired results. Wishful thinking, threats, pep talks, platitudes, and incentives are not a substitute for preparing a work unit to perform effectively. Ask yourself this question: Have I ever been asked to perform a job without prior notice, without the appropriate resources and information, and without the proper skills? Most people will answer yes, adding that this is just part of what happens in the rapidly changing workplace. To this we would agree. The problem occurs when an organization or operation allows the practice of not being prepared to become a lifestyle rather than an aberration or occasional occurrence. Let's revisit another enterprise from our research to illustrate this point.

Unprepared to Do Battle

A large distribution center in the Midwest is responsible for filling orders for retail customers from its enormous warehouse operation. The center operates twenty-four hours a day using three shifts. Warehouse staff are responsible for filling a certain number of customer orders each shift by a certain time, with the right products being properly loaded on the right trucks for delivery to customers in a four-state area. The operation is in trouble, and a performance audit reveals its magnitude: the accuracy of filling customer orders is poor, customer orders are being damaged in transit, and trucks are unable to stick to delivery schedules because the orders are not being completed on time. An operational analysis further reveals poor planning at the start of each shift in terms of prioritizing orders (with the result that shifts get off to a slow start), use of short staffing shifts to reduce labor costs, use of untrained temporary workers to augment the regular workforce (to further reduce labor costs), a lack of forklifts, which are needed to move customer orders, and inexperienced and ineffective front-line supervision. If things don't change quickly, the operation's future is in jeopardy.

The managers of this facility were good, hardworking people but, as a management team, they allowed themselves to develop some very bad habits, and these had a debilitating effect on the performance of their people and operation as a whole. They operated in a less than optimal fashion until little problems and occasional bad habits became an operational lifestyle. This particular operation failed to prepare itself for battle, and now its people were fighting for their working lives. and the survival of their business.

So what does it mean to properly prepare for battle? The answer is different for every manager because it is based on the needs of each operation and a host of situational variables. But managers in this research identified four key practices to prepare for battle (Figure 3.1). While the term *preparing for battle* might seem a bit dramatic, for people "just going to work" the word picture is poignant and worth remembering, because to be unprepared to compete today simply doesn't make good business sense.

Here are the four key practices:

- Develop and implement systematic planning practices on a variety of levels so that surprises and chaos become the exception rather than the rule.
- Practice progressive staffing to ensure that your operation has the right people, in the right positions, with the right

Figure 3.1. Preparing for Battle: Four Critical Practices

skills, at the right time. These practices include effective human resource planning, excellent selection practices, and effective work schedules.

- Ensure that all personnel are properly trained to perform their jobs and are being educated to "think like business-people."
- Ensure that your people have the tools, equipment, technology, information, and resources they need to get their jobs done.

Collectively, these commonsense practices prepare an operation to get desired results. But they require a leader who is willing to take the preparation component of the job very seriously. When we asked managers why preparation is not taken more seriously by their peers, the following themes emerged:

An overreliance on the "get it done regardless of the circum-
stances" belief.
Failing to take the time to prepare.
Having more immediate and pressing problems to deal with.
Not fully appreciating the importance of preparation.
Feeling their control is limited by the organization's policies and
procedures.
Lack of empathy for their people.

Although all of these issues might be plausible in certain
select situations, none address the fundamental issue that our
managers considered to be critically important: Are you properly prepared to achieve the results you so desperately need to
be successful?

■ **Practice 1: Develop and Use
Systematic and Ongoing Planning Practices**

IRREFUTABLE PERFORMANCE PRINCIPLE: Effective planning is not optional for results-oriented leaders because rapidly changing organizations need systemic future thinking
more than ever.

Several years ago we interviewed a CEO of a large service organization that was experiencing rapid change. We asked him
which thinking skills had the biggest impact on performance.
He quickly responded, "That's an obvious thing for us. It is
planning skills and the discipline to plan, because managers here
must be visualizing and preparing for the future, whether we
are talking about this afternoon, or next week, month, quarter,
or year. . . . Otherwise they will always be at the mercy of the unforgiving, unforeseen, and unanticipated." What really struck
us was that he emphasized not just having effective planning

skills but having the discipline to plan. In fact, his enterprise had a reputation for effective planning at all levels to avoid being "at the mercy of the unforgiving, unforeseen, and unanticipated."

The Importance of Effective Planning

As a manager, it's important to have a clearly defined mission and specific goals for your work unit, whether that happens to be the entire enterprise, a division, a department, or a work team. Planning is your decision-making and "future thinking" process. Through it you determine how to accomplish your mission and achieve your goals. Quite simply, *planning* means formulating a course of future action. You will use your plan of action to direct the behavior, activities, and resource deployment of your operation. As we all know, in theory planning goes like this: Ready, Aim, Fire. In reality, most managers know that it's all too easy to pull the trigger without proper preparation and focus. In that case, planning goes like this: Fire, Ready, Aim. Our purpose here is not to provide a detailed discussion of all the facets and nuisances of the planning process but rather to sensitize you to the importance of effective planning in your current position. The managers in our study provided us with some excellent insight on planning—but first a quick review.

Open up any book on management, leadership, and planning and the author will inevitably provide the reader with a model of the planning process. These types of models are usually quite similar, addressing the need to analyze your situation, set clear goals and objectives, and develop action plans. Once plans have been developed they must be implemented and monitored for effectiveness and then feedback must be used to make adjustments in the process to keep things moving in the right direction. A straightforward enough process in theory—but not necessarily in practice when managers at all levels of the organization are moving at breakneck speed. However, an organization's ability to achieve desired results is predicated on the effective implementation of a systematic planning process by managers (at all levels) and their ability to communicate effectively with others they need to implement specific action plans.

Here is an exercise to answer the following question: *As a leader, do you possess the skills necessary to conduct effective planning for your level in your organization, and are you organized in your approach to planning?* Find a quiet time and place (which requires planning), and answer each of these questions:

Find Out Now—Do You Plan for Success?

1. What type of planning is most important to my job?
2. What planning skills do I need to improve upon?
3. Am I taking adequate time for planning on a regular basis?
4. What happens to planning when I get too busy?
5. What planning activities do my people need from me to get their work done?
6. Does my boss provide me with the direction and information I need to develop effective plans? If not, what am I going to do about it?

The answers to these questions are critically important for any manager interested in improving results. And while platitudes abound—like "Those who fail to plan, plan to fail" or "Remember: Poor planning produces pitifully poor performance"—some might argue that these days, managers who have demonstrated planning prowess are in short supply.

Research in the psychological sciences (and common sense) tells us that when people get too busy, a number of negative things happen to their cognitive processes. Extremely busy people frequently tend to stop listening. They limit their talk with others, think short term, and fail to notice the things going on around them.[1] And while following such patterns might simply be human nature, for a manager (at any level) these are pathological behaviors. Having said these things, do you know of any manager (yourself included) who is *not* extremely busy?

Most managers we know are busier than they would like to be; it is a predicament that opens the door to planning problems.

Eight Common Planning Mistakes to Avoid

Our interviews with hundreds of managers in this study revealed a pattern of mistakes in planning that can be traced back to numerous causes, among them "human nature" and simply failing to develop effective planning habits. Here is a list of common fatal flaws in planning:

- Being too busy or too undisciplined to plan.
- Doing the wrong kinds of planning for your level in the organization.
- Planning with inadequate information and input from your boss.
- Planning in a vacuum without input from those who have to implement the plan.
- Developing plans that are unrealistic or too sophisticated to get off the ground.
- Failing to implement plans.
- Planning without accurate data.
- Planning without a clear direction or real purpose.

These eight mistakes are common in planning, and they are thus a good place for you to start a self-review as a manager. So what should you do to improve your planning effectiveness?

- Start every facet of the planning process with this thought: "What results are we really trying to achieve here?"
- Identify the level and type of planning that you must be engaged in to be effective and make sure that you are asking the appropriate questions for the type of planning you are doing. Know your environment and the planning needs of your operation.

- Develop your planning model to include analyzing your situation, setting clear goals and objectives, developing action plans, implementing and monitoring those plans for effectiveness, and providing feedback. Remember that your planning model must meet the demands of your situation and the needs of your people.

- Identify which actions you need to take to lead the planning process in your operation, and determine when you need to perform them. Make these actions part of your performance script. Don't forget about the most important level of planning—personal planning for the use of your time and energy.

- Develop an appropriate planning cycle. Use it to review, update, and implement your plans on a regular basis, then use feedback to improve both the plans themselves and the process you used to create them.

- Get key people involved in your planning process. Obtain their input, their ideas, and their take on how realistic your plan is, and get their ownership of the process you are creating. It is important to remember that input from stakeholders is critical to your success.

- Be disciplined. Once you've created a planning process, you will need discipline to think ahead (despite the pressure to think short term) and discipline to "work the plan" once it has been developed.

Practical Example—Planning at a Manufacturing Facility

A manufacturing facility's productivity was falling through the floor. A work-processing review revealed that work for the production lines was being scheduled at the last minute, planning for staffing was an afterthought, critical production inventories were not monitored, job assignments were being made only minutes before the shift, and maintenance in the operation was crisis driven—preventive maintenance was nonexistent. A new plant manager worked with operation managers at all levels to develop a specific planning model that would address these issues on a regular basis. The outcome of this model was profound: The amount of time managers in this particular operation spent on planning went from ten minutes to two hours per shift; it became part and parcel of both their job description and incentive pay. In the words of one manager from this operation, "We went from chaos to order by building a planning process that worked for us and sticking to it. . . . It's a lot easier to come to work knowing what is coming at you." As can be seen from this example, successful preparation for battle always starts with a plan of action.

■ Practice 2: Use Progressive Staffing—Put People First

IRREFUTABLE PERFORMANCE PRINCIPLE: You cannot produce superior results when human resource planning, selection, and work scheduling do not receive the utmost attention.

As a result of competitive pressure to cut costs and restructuring, reengineering, and rightsizing efforts, managers are being asked (told) to do more with fewer people.[2] It is as simple as that! It is the equivalent of asking a symphony orchestra conductor to make better-sounding music with fewer percussionists and smaller string, woodwind, and brass sections. A tough job indeed, and it is being further compounded by a shortage of skilled and motivated workers in nearly every segment of the labor market.

Progressive staffing is much more than simply filling a vacant or new position. Progressive staffing focuses on all facets of keeping the right number of the right people in the right jobs at the right time. This requires that a manager develop great prowess in human resource planning, selection, and scheduling processes. And these processes are filled with pitfalls, which can include failing to anticipate turnover, over- or understaffing an operation, not knowing the requirements of jobs, recruiting from too small a pool of candidates, ineffective selection procedures, and failing to take great care in developing work schedules.

A recent study by John Pfeffer and John Veiga, "Putting People First for Organizational Success," found that high-performance organizations paid painstaking attention to all facets of the staffing and selection process, a practice that translated into improved shareholder value.[3] This great care manifests itself in progressive staffing practices to ensure that the organization brings in the best people available and does not compromise its standards. High-performance managers know that ineffective staffing and compromised selection standards create situations that managers almost always regret in the long run. The adage "Anything worth doing is worth doing well" definitely applies here.

Here's an exercise to answer the question: *Do you take great care to ensure that your operation is properly staffed by people who can achieve the results you desire?* Mark the following statements with 1, 2, or 3 to indicate whether you perform those activities (1) to a limited extent, (2) to some extent, or (3) to a great extent.

Find Out Now—Are You Staffing for Results?

1. I plan so as to anticipate turnover and our future personnel needs.   _____
2. I work to make sure our operation has the right number and right kind of people.   _____
3. I analyze the requirements of a job before beginning the selection process.   _____
4. I have a clear picture of the skills necessary to perform each job effectively.   _____
5. We use multiple selection procedures (hurdles) to identify the best people.   _____
6. We adhere to equal employment opportunity guidelines.   _____
7. We ultimately select people based on their ability to get results.   _____
8. I develop work schedules that help meet the needs of the operation and my people.   _____

Any statement you marked with a 1 or a 2 is an area that needs attention and improvement, because these statements represent the heart of progressive staffing. They can be boiled down into three key functions:

- Planning and anticipating staffing changes.
- Developing and employing effective selection hurdles.
- Taking great care in developing work schedules.

Plan and Anticipate Staffing Needs

As a manager, you need to know how many people are needed to get the work done. Your goal should be to have the supply of labor equal the demand. Having too many people is problematic for your bottom line. Also, having too few people can damage quality, customer service, morale, and results. To illustrate, if you are like most managers and have, say, four people working for you, you probably need six (and if your organization deemed it necessary, it might give you three to do that same work). Therefore this means that extreme care must be taken in properly selecting and utilizing the people you have been given by your organization.

Thinly staffed organizations need to take great care in anticipating both growth needs and turnover, simply because of lag times associated with needing people, finding people, and having people ready to be productive.[4] The overwhelming majority of managers in our studies find their units understaffed. Therefore planning and anticipating staffing changes is a necessary part of most managers' lives. And doing so goes a long way toward maintaining and increasing performance. When you plan for expansions and increased labor needs, you do a more effective job of finding the right people and getting them to be productive sooner.

The selection process can always be viewed as a series of "hurdles" that the candidate must clear to stay in the hiring race.[5] When you are hiring people, you need to be very effective at developing meaningful hurdles for candidates. Meaningful hurdles increase the likelihood of bringing the best quality people into your organization. Here are the five hurdles that managers frequently describe as necessary for effective selection:

Hurdle 1: Résumé and Application Form Review
Hurdle 2: Interviews
Hurdle 3: Formal Testing
Hurdle 4: Reference Checking
Hurdle 5: Physical Examination

Each hurdle must be handled with extreme care to identify the best candidate while being aware of and complying with equal employment opportunity concerns. Although all of these hurdles are important, you have the greatest control over hurdles 1 and 2.

Hurdle 1: Résumé and Application Form Review
Review the résumé and application form information to avoid wasting time on candidates who do not even meet the acceptable standards for the job in question! In reviewing the information provided by both the résumé and a completed application form, watch for the following potential concerns and applicant weaknesses:

Sketchy and erratic job history
Time gaps, which may indicate job, personality, personal, or
    physical or mental problems
Salary or wages and benefits requirements are very different
    from what the job offers

Over- or underqualification (experience, education) for the job
being applied for

Negative reasons for leaving previous employment (for example, personality conflicts, didn't like the work or the organization, was fired or demoted)

Hurdle 2: Interview

The cornerstone of most selection processes is the selection interview. Here's how to implement it successfully:

Prepare for the Interview. Results-oriented managers take several preparatory steps before the scheduled interview:

1. Review the job description and the job specifications.
2. Study the application form and résumé and check with the
   references named there.
3. Determine areas of inquiry and questions you want to ask.
4. Arrange appropriate surroundings.
5. Allocate enough time for the interview.

Taking these preparatory steps smooths your way so that,
for example, you've read the résumé or job application form
ahead of time and refer to it only when necessary. Also, most
people when interviewed have questions of their own. Here are
four common questions to anticipate and deal with early in the
interview:

- Why was I selected to be interviewed?
- How long it will take you to make the hiring decision?
- Will I hear anything about the outcome of the interview?
- If so, how, when, and from whom will I hear about the out-
  come of the interview?

Develop the Interview Format. Once you have prepared yourself for the interview, you are ready to plan the interview

process. Each selection interview should include these six sequential steps:

1. Start by introducing yourself, shaking hands, and welcoming the interviewee. Be aware of, and guard against, initial impressions and biases gained in the first four minutes (commonly referred to as the "Four-Minute Barrier") because these can seriously affect the remainder of the interview.
2. Engage in some relaxing, non–business-related conversation.
3. Obtain relevant information from the interviewee.
4. Provide information about, and sell the interviewee on, the organization.
5. Ask for and answer directly any questions the interviewee may have.
6. Conclude the interview.

Go over these steps in your mind until you're sure how you will approach each one. Pay particular attention to Step 3, as that's where you will get the information you need to make your choice. For further help, see the UMB series book *Strategic Interviewing,* by Richaurd Camp, Mary E. Vielhaber, and Jack L. Simonetti.

Conduct the Interview. In the third stage of the interview process, the actual conduct of the interview, the goal is to obtain as much relevant information as possible. Because the selection process is essentially a prediction decision, you must learn enough to help you determine which of the various candidates is best suited for the job being filled.

Making a hiring decision is similar to selecting a horse to bet on at a race track. Some people will buy a $3 racing form that lists all the horses scheduled to run in each race and then take the time to analyze each horse's qualifications. They'll study its race results—whether it runs well on a muddy or dry track, has finished no worse than third in the last eight races, runs well with this particular jockey, and so on—and then make a $2, $5, or $10 bet. Organizations and managers as interviewers are betting on an individual to be a winning employee at an annual salary of $30,000, $50,000, $75,000 and up. They have rather more need for relevant information than our horse-racing fans have—and yet sometimes they seem to do less information gathering and analysis!

You obtain information through the art and science of asking questions. Interviewing rests heavily upon techniques of questioning. When you use the right techniques, you can acquire access to information otherwise unavailable. Improperly handled, the interview becomes a source of serious bias because it may restrict access to, and even distort, information. One of the primary failures in communication during an interview is not getting, or allowing, the interviewee to talk. As the interviewer, your best strategy is to listen more and talk less. Thus, on average, the interviewee should talk about 75 percent of the time and you should talk about 25 percent of the time.

After the employment interview, the interviewee should know more than that "someone will be in touch" later. Who? When? By telephone? Letter? Too often, even professional interviewers fail to provide a thorough orientation toward the next step. Because many interviewees may be too timid to inquire, the interview is apt to end on a sour note instead of a positive one. When you close the interview, make sure that you both know where you're going from here. In this way, the interviewee is left with a positive image of both the interviewer and the organization.

Hurdle 3: Formal Testing

The third hurdle to be cleared by the job applicant are the formal tests that have been developed in an effort to find a more objective means of measuring qualifications, as well as for use with employees who are candidates for transfer or promotion.

One of the major advantages of formal tests are that they may uncover qualifications and talent that would not be detected by interviews or by the listing of education and job experience on an application form or résumé. These tests seek to eliminate the possibility that the prejudice of the interviewer or manager—instead of the potential ability of the candidate—will govern selection decisions. There are various types of formal tests that can be employed. These include performance tests, aptitude and intelligence tests, interest tests, and personality and psychological tests. As a result, many highly effective organizations have found that such properly designed and administered tests have helped them in selecting better personnel, and that a professionally developed test has often been the best defense against allegations of employment discrimination.

Hurdle 4: Reference Checking

The fourth major hurdle to be considered as a part of the selection process is the checking of an applicant's references. The importance of a thorough check of the applicant's prior work and educational experience cannot be emphasized enough. It is an indispensable part of effective selection. Unfortunately, many managers are reluctant to put in the time and effort needed to check an applicant's prior work and education record properly. A self-imposed defeatist attitude on the part of the manager may lead to the feeling that an honest, thorough, and accurate response would probably not be forthcoming from the candidate's past employers anyway. This is an unfortunate decision. More often than not, time and effort put into reference checking pays big dividends. The manager often gains highly valuable and useful information related to the applicant's past work experience. In fact, until this type of check takes place, the manager has little or no idea of the validity of the information provided by the applicant on the application form and résumé or in the interview. The most commonly used methods of checking references are to use the telephone, the mails, face-to-face requests, or some combination of these methods.

Hurdle 5: Physical Examination

Good physical health is becoming more and more important today as a result of the escalation of health care benefit costs and workers' compensation claims that organizations are required to pay. The physical examination has gained even more importance after the introduction of the Americans with Disabilities Act (ADA). This law goes beyond banning discrimination against qualified workers with disabilities. It also directs employers to make reasonable accommodations, defined as not creating undue hardship for the employee, such as modifying workstations or providing readers for the blind.

Evaluation and Decision

To complete the process, you go over all the information on the applicant that was gathered from the various hurdles and complete a summary rating. Table 3.1 provides summary rating criteria that can be used in this process to finalize your evaluation of each applicant. Make sure to provide supporting data for any conclusions listed about the applicant. This may be needed for legal purposes. Give particular attention to input about the applicant's strong and weak points as they pertain to the position.

Here are ten key P's that are frequently used by managers to evaluate an applicant and make a hire/no hire decision.

- *Promotion:* The interviewee's résumé, application form, and interview performance.
- *Product:* What the interviewee would be bringing to the job—skills, abilities, attitudes, values, and experience.
- *Package:* The overall appearance presented—dress, grooming, and posture.
- *Place:* The interviewee's willingness to relocate and travel.
- *Price:* The interviewee's asking price in terms of salary or wages and fringe benefits.
- *Preparation:* The interviewee's knowledge of the organization, its products and services, and the job being applied for.

Table 3.1. Summary Rating for Job Candidates

1. Outstanding	Applicant possesses all the necessary qualifications and has virtually no undesirable characteristics.
2. Very Good	Applicant is well qualified, but not outstanding, and my be expected to perform quite well on the job in spite of some minor deficiencies on basic abilities, personal characteristics, or character traits. Since these limitations are minor, however, they do not pose a problem.
3. Average	In most respects, this applicant is average. Only in the absence of a better candidate should a job offer be considered.
4. Fair	This is a marginal or borderline applicant about whom there is some serious doubt with regard to ability to perform satisfactorily. As a result, this person should be rejected in favor of a better candidate.
5. Unqualified	This applicant is unsatisfactory. The candidate is seriously deficient in one or more of the critical qualifications for the position and must be rejected, regardless of the need to fill the job.

- *Positive Attitude:* The interviewee should be upbeat, self-confident, and enthusiastic, as these qualities tend to carry over into performance on the job.
- *Personality:* The personality that the interviewee projects. Look for voice quality, good eye contact, a firm handshake, a ready smile, and good manners.
- *Persistence:* The persistence of the interviewee in going after the job.
- *Performance—Putting It All Together:* Has the interviewee performed well enough in putting all the first nine key P's together to be a top-quality job candidate?

Remember that results-oriented managers take extreme care in all facets of the selection process, but particularly in interviewing.

Develop Effective Work Schedules

The scheduling of work may or may not be a huge factor in your unit. Still, most results-oriented managers take great care to ensure that work schedules help maximize performance and meet the growing needs of their employees. The growth of such practices as flextime, job sharing, condensed work weeks, twenty-four-hour continuous operations, telecommuting, and comp time can place tremendous pressure on managers to make wise work scheduling decisions when they are already working thin staffed. A lack of day care, the need for vacations and family leave, and the abundance of dual working parents all make work scheduling important. Successful managers balance concern for their people with concern for getting desired results and this concern manifests itself in work schedules that work for both the employee and the organization.

Practical Example—
Getting Serious About Progressive Staffing

Mary's organization had always been an employer of choice in her community and potential employees would come in to seek employment. Her organization had the pick of the litter in terms of selecting the best employees in the area. In the past the manager's role in the selection process of new employees was fairly limited, almost nonexistent in some cases. Mary's large division was now experiencing staffing problems for the first time because of increased competition and a tightening of the local labor market. Newly hired employees assigned to her division were not as strong in terms of their knowledge, skills, and attitudes as in the past and her operation's performance was starting to slip. After a conversation with the human resource director to voice her concern over the diminished quality of new employees she received a follow-up e-mail message. The human resources director again explained the cause of the problem, ending the message with the sarcastic comment, "Mary, if you think you can do better, go for it!"

Mary gladly accepted the challenge and for the first time became intimately involved with the human resource department in every facet of the recruiting and selection process. She had a mission to recruit the best people possible, and she wanted to expand the pool of qualified candidates and to play an active part in improving selection procedures so as to weed out people incapable of achieving the desired level of performance. Several months into the process a peer approached Mary and said, "How do you find the time to be so involved in the selection process with all your other duties?" Mary's response was very telling: "We are only as good as the people we have working with us so if we are going to hit these big numbers we can't afford any more 'bad hires'—and I am not willing any longer to leave that to chance or to the HR people exclusively! . . . Without good people my career could be in jeopardy."

■ Practice 3: Train and Educate Your Staff

> IRREFUTABLE PERFORMANCE PRINCIPLE: Properly trained and educated personnel increase the likelihood of achieving desired levels of performance, while untrained personnel can create countless problems for an organization.

A critical component of being prepared for battle is having your people properly trained to perform their jobs effectively. In addition, results-oriented managers tend to go one step further. They have a willingness and commitment to educate their people so that the whole group tends to think more like owners, salespeople, and managers than like people isolated in one part of the organization. The catch is that both of these activities take time and effort, yet study after study reveal that training creates competitive advantage. And the importance of effective and timely training is only increasing because of downsizing, the explosion of technology in the workplace, empowerment, work teams, the tight labor market, and oftentimes the lack of high-quality graduates ready to fill entry-level positions.

Although the necessity for effective training has gone up, the commitment to training can easily be pushed aside by monetary concerns, as in this scenario: A CFO approaches a division general manager with a very perturbed look and says, "We can't spend this much on workforce training! What if we train 'em and they leave?" The general manager calmly looks back at the CFO and asks, "What if we don't train 'em and they stay?"

Here's an exercise to answer the question: *Are your people properly trained to perform their value-added job, and have they been educated to think like business people?* Mark the following statements with 1, 2, or 3 to indicate whether you perform those activities (1) to a limited extent, (2) to some extent, or (3) to a great extent.

Find Out Now—Is Training Really a Priority?

1. Employee training is a top priority. _____
2. My employees are properly trained to excel in their jobs. _____
3. My work unit has developed specific skill sets for each position. _____
4. My work unit has developed training plans for employees to ensure effective learning. _____
5. My organization budgets time and money to ensure effective employee learning. _____
6. My operation practices effective on-the-job training. _____
7. I encourage and reward managers and employees to be active and effective trainers of those needing training. _____
8. I effectively monitor and assess the performance of trainees. _____

9. I provide coaching and performance
    feedback to trainees.   _____

10. My organization is educating employees
    to think like businesspeople.   _____

Any statement you marked with a 1 or a 2 is an area that needs attention and improvement, because of their impact on employee learning.

To explore the consequences of having a poorly trained workforce, we recently surveyed a large sample of managers and asked them two questions:

- What are the organizational and individual consequences of having poorly trained personnel?
- What are the primary reasons why organizations fail to properly train their people?

The key findings to each of these questions are listed in hierarchical order in Table 3.2.

Table 3.2. Consequences and Causes of Ineffective Training Practices

Consequences

Organizational	Individual
1. Poor productivity	1. Increased frustration and stress
2. Quality problems	2. Loss of motivation
3. Customer dissatisfaction	3. Ineffective performance
4. Poor morale and bad attitudes	4. Loss of confidence or self-esteem
5. Loss of teamwork and cooperation	5. Job dissatisfaction

Primary Reasons

1. Training is not a management priority
2. Lack of time to properly train employees
3. Overreliance on on-the-job or trial-and-error learning
4. Assume the individual is already competent
5. Unclear on skill set needed to perform the job

A review of Table 3.2 reveals that the organizational and individual consequences of ineffective training practices are results busters at the organizational performance level, in that productivity quality and customer service slide while morale and teamwork suffer.[6] Individually, workers experience increased frustration and stress, a loss of motivation, ineffective performance, a loss of confidence, and job dissatisfaction. What sane manager would wish to encounter these outcomes? Yet the reasons for these problems are telling.

Why Make Training a Priority?

Unless managers make training a priority and train effectively, problems are inevitable. When managers simply throw people into jobs or assume the job-holder knows what to do and how to do it, they are asking for less than optimal performance. Finally, when managers are unclear about the skill set necessary to perform the job, training suffers. Would a manager who is truly interested in getting results allow these things to happen? Our position is that it can happen to anyone who gets busy enough or pressed hard enough for short-term results. Training is a lot like shaving, if you don't do it for a couple of days you don't look too bad, but in the long term you really start to look shabby without proper grooming.

Develop a Systems Approach to Training and Education

Training and development are responsibilities jointly shared between a line manager and people in various support functions (such as human resource, information technology, and engineering). Still, the ultimate burden of ensuring that people are properly prepared to perform rests on their direct supervisor. Results-oriented leaders tend to approach training and education from a systems perspective. The systems approach forces organizations and managers to think through the practice of training workers and can be helpful in removing the causes of ineffective training. The six steps in this process, evolved from the input of effective managers, are as follows:

Step 1: Develop a Clear and Flexibly Framed Job Description. Without a job description that is easy to understand and to interpret in the light of changing job requirements, effective job training becomes very difficult at best. An effective job description will contain the specific tasks and responsibilities that the job incumbent is expected to perform to provide value to the organization. Flexibly framed job descriptions can be developed by a manager and subordinate, or a group of subordinates working together, or even a job analyst. An effective job description is the road map for all training activities. All training efforts should be aimed at preparing the employee to perform the duties of the job effectively, and this cannot happen unless duties have been clearly defined.

Step 2: Identify a Specific Skill Set for Each Job. Once the job description has been developed, a simple question is in order: What knowledge, skills, and abilities (KSAs) does an employee need to perform the job effectively? Often, employees are poorly trained because managers fail to clearly identify the specific KSAs necessary to perform a job (that is, job specifications). Job specifications can be defined in several ways: by human resource specialists conducting effective job analysis, by the individual employee and/or employee focus groups, by manager-subordinate discussions, or by a combination of these.

The skill set identification step shows the employee what knowledge is required for effectiveness in the job. The more complex the job, the more complex the skill set. Once a specific skill set has been established, the training process can proceed in a focused fashion. Without a clear understanding of the KSAs required for effective performance, any training effort is hard-pressed to produce desired results.

Step 3: Establish Specific Learning Objectives. Once the job specifications have been clarified, you can establish specific learning objectives for an employee. Learning objectives represent specific targets for the trainee. For example, a receptionist might have the learning objective of becoming proficient at transferring incoming phone calls and using established telephone etiquette procedures. A machine operator could be given the learning objective of finding out how to calibrate various types of machines effectively. The key here is to articulate in no uncertain terms specific learning targets that are tied to desired results.

Clarify short-term and long-term learning objectives for your employees. Doing so allows them to excel in their jobs. In contrast, to fail to establish meaningful learning objectives is to invite large performance gaps into the workplace, with all the corresponding negative consequences. Simply telling employees what they must know to be effective is a powerful learning device.

Step 4: Develop and Implement a Training Plan of Action. Once learning objectives have been established, develop a specific training plan to help employees learn. Human resources can be your ally in developing such a plan. Off-the-job and on-the-job training methods must be considered. Off-the-job training methods can include seminars, workshops, tutorials, computer-assisted training, coaching and mentoring sessions, and self-study programs, among others. Ninety percent of all training takes place on the job, using such methods as job instructional training, on-the-spot coaching and mentoring, cross-training, job aides, and performance scripts. The important point is that these activities be articulated and developed into a learning plan that can be implemented systematically. Simply throwing an employee into a job sends all the wrong messages and increases the likelihood of failure and frustration. Enlist coworkers to help you develop and implement a training plan, especially if they are able and willing to assist in training. Without effective implementation and a blend of on-the-job and off-the-job methods, employee learning is suspect.

Step 5: Provide Ongoing Assessment and Performance Feedback. All trainees want to know how well they are doing during a training process, program, or period. Effective training systems provide an ongoing assessment of employee performance and appropriate feedback to reinforce desired performance and corrective action for less than acceptable performance. Assessment and feedback are the keys to effective learning and should be linked to the job description, learning objectives, and training plans. In many organizations the absence of effective feedback keeps employees from knowing how well they are performing. For the trainee, this can create fear, uncertainty, doubt, and even paranoia, all of which have a negative impact on the learning process. Assessment and feedback can come from self-review, trainers, and immediate supervisors. The key is to provide trainees with meaningful, ongoing feedback from knowledgeable sources. Without this step, the learning process fails to create closure for the trainee. In many organizations, assessment and feedback are the missing pieces in the training system.

Step 6: Educating People to Understand Their Impact on Performance. Once people have been trained on how to perform their jobs effectively, results-oriented managers will help them understand the big picture of performance. Ask yourself this question: Do my people think like owners and businesspeople? If they haven't been educated to understand how your business operates and makes money, then you are missing a key component that influences behavior. The practice of *open book management,* sharing performance and operating data with all members of the organization, is growing rapidly—but it only works if people have been educated to understand this information.

Results-oriented leaders educate their people to understand, at a minimum, these five key performance issues:

- How do we attract and keep our customers?
- What do our performance measures really mean?
- How does our organization make money?
- What factors currently affect our operating performance?
- How does my job affect our organization's performance?

Research on open-book management makes it clear that when employees understand the big picture and their role in an organization's performance it can have a very powerful effect on their behavior and performance.[7]

Practical Example—Preparing Leaders to Lead

A *Fortune* 500 organization faced a serious challenge in that the business was changing faster than its managers at all levels could keep up with. Following a trend not uncommon to many organizations these days, new managers were frequently placed in positions with little or no preparation—with less than desirable results. Incumbent managers received surprisingly little in the way of development to improve their skills and performance with the same outcome. The officers of this enterprise recognized the problem and set out to correct it in a very systematic and thorough fashion. First, they created a cross-functional management development team (MDT) responsible to move the process forward and provide financial resources and sanction for this high-profile activity. Second, the MDT created a managerial skill set for all managers in the organization that would be needed both now and in the future. Third, they established a comprehensive management training and development process that focused on assessment, education, on-the-job experience, coaching, and performance appraisal and review. Fourth, top management made management training and development a top priority in both word and deed. And finally, managers at all levels were held accountable for the training and development of their subordinate managers in implementing this process.[8] In the words of this organization's CEO, "If training and developing our managers is not a top priority, then we are not really serious about the survival and continued success of this organization. . . . Any manager seeking better performance from the people around them had better make sure that people are trained to do their jobs and to do them well."

■ **Practice 4: Equip People with
the Tools They Need to Perform**

> IRREFUTABLE PERFORMANCE PRINCIPLE: When people
> are properly equipped with the right performance tools, they
> can better focus on getting desired results.

In the rush to get things done at work, it is not uncommon to see people being asked to perform increasingly complex tasks without the performance tools they need. We consider *performance tools* to include equipment, technology, information, authority, supplies, and the materials needed to get the job done appropriately. Sometimes the tools people need to get better results cost thousands of dollars—like better heavy equipment or the latest piece of technology or a reconfigured work station. Other times, the tools people need to improve their performance cost little or nothing—as in the case of accurate information, a computer access code, or even something as simple as an ample supply of rubber gloves and pencils.

Equipping your people with the performance tools they need to get the performance you need used to be easier than it is today. In the past many managers were promoted up through the ranks, so they had a clear idea of what tools were needed to get the job done. This was because they had actually performed many of these jobs themselves, and the jobs were so stable that the things currently needed for performance were the same as the ones that were needed in their pre-management days. Today many managers are being asked to lead and support people who are in jobs which the manager does not fully understand (or in many cases fully appreciate). A manager recently illustrated the issue when she commented to us, "I have no clue what these people do in their jobs. I only know what output we need from them." This means that managers need to take special steps to ensure that their people have the tools they need to get the job done in spite of a possibly limited understanding of what it actually requires.

We could provide numerous examples of the problems managers and organizations create for themselves because they fail to engage their people in the simple process of determining what performance tools are needed to get optimal results. A recent experience illustrates the importance of this practice. We were doing work in a large community hospital that was struggling to contain costs. Unit directors were ordered to cut costs wherever they deemed appropriate. In short order, supplies of rubber gloves, Post-it notes, tape, straws, gauze, clips, and a host of other apparently trivial things began to dwindle to the point where medical people in the units were angry and frustrated by the fact that they didn't have these simple tools at their fingertips.

Because those doing the cutting failed to appreciate the importance of these specific items, productivity, morale and patient care began to suffer. This cost containment could have been implemented much more effectively if the directors had engaged those doing the work in the process of determining what was needed to do the work while controlling costs.

To find if your people are properly equipped to perform their jobs, ask several of them to answer the following questions, then follow up with one-on-one discussions with them.

Find Out Now—Is Your Operation Equipped for Results?

1. What additional information do you need that will help performance?
2. What additional equipment do you need that will help performance?
3. What additional technology do you need that will help performance?
4. What additional supplies or material do you need that will help performance?
5. Do you have the authority or sanction you need to get your job done?

It is our experience that operations that are struggling rarely pay close attention to the performance tools issue because they are focusing on matters that appear larger or more urgent. One wonders what is more critical at a basic level than providing the tools people need to do their work well. To not provide the necessary performance tools at a satisfactory level is to invite less than satisfactory performance.

Develop a Toolbox Checklist

When preparing for battle, ensuring that people are equipped with the right tools is particularly important. Managers in our research classified the "big five tools" needed to get results and to avoid the costs of being unprepared. When people do not have the *information* they need the outcomes can be miscommunication, miscues, and mistakes. When *equipment* and *technology* are not in place, lost productivity and inefficiencies become commonplace. Without appropriate *materials and supplies* people waste time and effort waiting, looking, and doing without. Finally, without appropriate *levels of authority* that should come with being empowered, people get frustrated and lose their willingness to push hard to get things done.

Managers need to be very approachable on the issue of the specific things people need to get the job done. An effective leader will regularly ask people what additional resources they need to improve their performance and will take appropriate steps to get them what they need. Our interviews with hundreds of managers made it clear that this is frequently a hard habit to develop in times of cost containment and doing more with less but clearly one worth pursuing. Managers repeatedly spoke of the importance of developing a systematic checklist of the "toolbox resources" that were needed by employees to get results. Once the list is developed, effective managers do what they need to do to ensure that people have the tools they need and are empowered to better equip themselves in the future.

Practical Example—
A Large Trucking Facility's Toolbox Checklist

A large trucking facility was plagued by inefficiencies, bad morale, and poor quality of service. The organization was embarking on developing empowered work teams in their operation and set up an "improvement council" to spearhead this effort. At the very first meeting there was an explosion of frustration over the fact that workers felt management sent them to work unequipped on a daily basis. The following is the to-do list of what workers thought needed to be fixed before anything else could happen:

- Provide more accurate information on what trailers need to be unloaded.
- Repair broken computer keyboards.
- Replace scanning wands for bar codes.
- Replace missing dock hooks for opening trailers.
- Provide sharpened pencils to complete paperwork.
- Keep a supply of manifests and needed documents.
- Make sure keys for forklifts are not missing.
- Provide an adequate supply of work gloves.
- Have plastic wrap for bundling orders.
- Have brooms on the dock to sweep trailers.

The majority of these issues focused clearly on creating a toolbox checklist to equip employees with the tools they needed to get desired results. And although any one of these issues might be viewed as no more important than a grain of sand on the beach, collectively they were the whole beach to these workers who were being asked to improve their performance. When leaders don't provide the right tools, the leaders' credibility is called into question and the workers have a host of legitimate excuses for not doing great work.

CHAPTER SUMMARY

Preparing for battle is all about dealing with the myriad of important issues and details that include planning, staffing, training and educating, and equipping your operation to perform and perform well. When these issues are not taken seriously and dealt with systematically by a leader, the leader's overall performance and credibility both suffer. Results-oriented leaders make preparation a critical component of their game plan to improve performance, and they do so systematically. The cost of being unprepared for battle can be significant for modern managers. Lack of preparation for battle can cause performance to suffer, which can cause results to suffer—which will cause a manager's career to suffer. In the end there is no substitute for preparation if a manager is serious about improving performance. The words of Abraham Lincoln ring true here: "If I had six hours to cut down a tree I'd spend four hours sharpening my axe." So as you embark on your pursuit of better performance it is of the utmost importance that your axe is sharp enough to get the level of performance you are seeking.

Absolute #3

Stoke the Fire of Performance: Create a Climate for Results

A corporate executive of a large retailing organization recently said something that might serve as a warning to anyone in a leadership position: "For the last six months all I've been doing is going to meetings and writing cockamamy restructuring reports that I doubt anyone even reads. . . . In my heart I know that I am not creating value for our shareholders and I am so busy that I am not helping my people create value, either." In other words, this manager is busy. But—to return to the question asked in Chapter Two—busy doing what?

A successful general manager from a pharmaceutical company gives us a rich word picture of what he considers to be a critical results-oriented behavior: "I sort of look at my job as an engineer on a steam locomotive. . . . I've got to keep the train on the tracks and keep looking ahead, while at the same time stoking the fire to keep moving toward our goal." The notion of "stoking the fire" suggests that this manager has to provide the appropriate fuel at the appropriate level and time and then ensure that things don't burn so hot as to consume all those involved or so cool that things don't get done. This word picture suggests the importance of creating a climate for achievement. Although the retailing manager was busy, his day-to-day activity was not providing his operation with the fuel it needed to increase its performance. This is a common pitfall for modern managers.

In Chapter Two we discussed the importance of clarifying one's role in the organization. At this point we would like to add several practices that, based on our research, are critical to stoking the fires of performance. But first, let's look at an example of what can happen to a manager who fails to create a climate for achievement.

The Leader Who Wasn't

Bob, a thirty-three-year-old chemical engineer with an MBA from an excellent business school, was manager of a small processing plant that produced a variety of specialty chemicals. The facility operated twenty-four hours a day, seven days a week, with three shifts of twenty people. There were two supervisors per shift, all six of whom had more experience than Bob did. The plant had been performing marginally at best when Bob took the job, and by the time he'd been there a little over eighteen months, costs were out of control and a host of little problems were becoming big problems. Even though performance goals and plans were in place, performance feedback was nonexistent and people felt that Bob was completely out of touch with the operation. There was a general sense that the workforce was unmotivated and pretty much did whatever they wanted whenever they wanted. Problems were generally left to boil over before they were addressed. While Bob's boss described him as "an empowerment person," his own people viewed him as "a wimp" who had lost control of his operation. Some twenty-nine months into his tenure as plant manager, Bob was demoted. He eventually left the organization.

Bob's great technical skills earned him his promotion into this key management position. Unfortunately, his management skills weren't up to the job. He failed to take charge and create a results-oriented performance climate, and things went from bad to worse.

In these days of empowerment, work teams, participative management, flat organizational structure, and virtual management, there is a fine line between being a "results-oriented leader" and being a "control freak." Yet the managers in our research made it clear that leaders must create a healthy tension and ongoing awareness around key issues of performance. Without a leader stoking the fire of performance at both the work unit and individual level, results can and will slide. It does little or no good to empower workers fresh from jobs in a failed business.

After a manager gets everyone in the operation on the same page in terms of what they are trying to achieve and what activities are most important, it becomes critical to prepare for battle. Then, once plans are in place and people are properly trained and equipped to perform, managers must stoke the fires of performance by creating a results-oriented climate through their leadership. Figure 4.1 sketches the interrelationships among the activities required for this process.

To this end, managers in this research identified four practices that are needed to increase performance. First, managers must stay in the know—that is stay aware of what is really going on around them in terms of performance, processes, and people. Second, managers must create ownership and accountability for desired results. That is to say, they must make it clear that results are not simply the

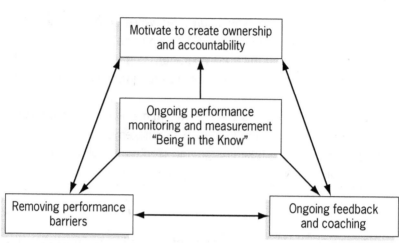

Figure 4.1. Stoking the Fire: Creating a Climate for Results

manager's concern but rather everyone's and that there is accountability for desired outcomes. Third, managers must develop a workplace climate where performance barriers are rapidly identified and removed so that performance is maximized and the manager's credibility is not eroded. Finally, results-oriented leaders provide ongoing performance feedback and coaching to their people about how to improve their performance. In the end, these performance-oriented practices become interconnected, and with time become difficult to separate from one other. When as a manager you do these things and do them well, you are stoking the fire of performance that is so critical to getting results. Interestingly, while these practices entail common sense, they are frequently uncommon in rapidly changing organizations.

■ Practice 1: Monitor and Measure Ongoing Performance

IRREFUTABLE PERFORMANCE PRINCIPLE: To lead effectively, you have to know how all facets of your operation are performing on an ongoing basis. This requires a balanced approach to monitoring and measuring individuals and work units in terms of behavior as well as results.

These days, managers are awash with information and data of every sort, from e-mail messages to on-line economic forecasts to productivity reports. In our interviews managers frequently stated (and rightfully complained) that they were being "overwhelmed," "buried," and "overloaded" with data made available by breakthroughs in information technology. Yet access to and possession of information does not necessarily translate into the critical managerial state of really knowing what is going on around you (what we call "being in the know"). And if managers don't really know what is going on around them, they cannot lead their operations to better results.

We've found that in highly successful organizations, managers tend to be closely linked to their operations and people. They tend to know what is really going on around them, and they use accurate and real information to guide their actions. Conversely, the managers of many struggling enterprises are frequently accused of being "clueless," "out of touch with reality," "operating in a vacuum," or being "in the dark" because they do not have their finger on the pulse of their operation and people. Once goals and plans have been established and performance expectations and roles have been clarified, a manager needs accurate performance information to take appropriate action to stoke the fires of performance.

The art of "being in the know" requires that managers possess the ability to monitor and measure performance so that they always know where current performance is in relation to desired performance standards. Being in the know goes beyond simply reviewing performance metrics or occasionally talking to a key employee or even conducting a formal performance appraisal. It requires that managers monitor and measure individual and work-unit performance on an ongoing basis. In this way, they can take corrective action when performance needs improvement, and reinforce, reward, and celebrate success when desired results happen. The importance of being in the know is underscored by the comments of one bank VP when she said, "Sometimes the performance of an operation suffers—which happens—but when the manager doesn't know they are struggling, it is completely unacceptable." For a leader to be able to stoke the fires of performance, it is essential to know where performance stands at the individual and work-unit level.

Here's an exercise to answer the question: *Do you monitor and measure the performance of your people and operation so that you know how things stand on an ongoing basis?*

Find Out Now—Are You in the Know?

1. Answer each of the questions in Worksheet 4.1.
2. Assess the degree to which your current approach allows you to be knowledgeable and accurate in your assessment of current performance in these areas.
3. Note down which areas need changes in order for you to be "in the know."

■ **Worksheet 4.1.** **Performance Monitoring Effectiveness** ■

Activity	Daily	Weekly	Monthly	Quarterly	Annually
1. How often do you observe the performance of individual employees in your operation?					
2. How often do you review the specific performance goals and measures of individual employees in your operation?					
3. How often do you observe the performance of your work unit in operation?					
4. How often do you review the performance metrics or scorecard of your work unit?					

The Four Categories for Measuring Performance

Managers in this research frequently described a balancing act between focusing on observable performance behaviors and hard performance measures on one hand and assessing individual versus overall work-unit performance on the other. A manager's orientation toward monitoring and measuring performance can be greatly affected by the nature of the work, the physical proximity of the staff, the nature of the delivery process, and the sophistication of the measurement system. But managers in this study made it clear that to be effective they must monitor and measure the performance of both individuals and the work unit by reviewing performance data and behavior on an ongoing basis.

To be in the know, these managers identified four categories for measuring performance. The matrix in Figure 4.2 indicates that being an effective manager requires that two sources of performance information must be known and understood at two different levels.

To this end, managers must master four critical practices that will determine the degree of success they experience in providing balance in monitoring and measuring performance:

	Observational Data	Measurement Data
Individual Performance	Interpersonal contact	Performance measurement review
Work Unit Performance	MBWA[3]	Scorecard review

Figure 4.2. **Monitoring and Measuring Performance Balance**

■ *Make interpersonal contact.* Observe the performance and behavior of your people regularly, and use interpersonal contact to keep in touch with them. This will soon become the norm rather than the exception. It also sets the stage for coaching employees, an important skill that will be discussed later.

■ *Measure individual performance.* At the same time, monitor and review individual measures of employee performance so that you know how well each individual is performing against the results you desire. In this way, you truly know what is going on at the individual employee level and you can add this information to your behavioral observations.

■ *Manage by walking around.* Interact regularly with the work unit, and manage by walking around—a practice we call MBWA-Cubed, or MBWA^3. MBWA is cubed because three activities are required: walking around, asking good questions (and listening to the answers), and answering any questions people may have. Make this contact ongoing but not predictable. In this way, you have a chance to interact informally while at the same time observing behavior and some of the activity of getting work done.

■ *Keep a scorecard.* Monitor and measure work unit performance against your previously established performance metrics or scorecard. In this way, you know what is going on in terms of overall results. The managers in our study made it clear that effective leaders track all four categories of performance and do so in a balanced and ongoing fashion.

Managers in this study told us they believed that most managers have an inclination toward monitoring and measuring a preferred type of performance (individual versus work unit), in a preferred fashion (observation versus performance data review), and that this prevents them from truly being in the know with their people and operation as a whole. Thus managers may lack a complete picture of performance and find themselves operating in a vacuum without even realizing it!

To prevent this from happening, ask yourself the following questions:

- Do I have accurate information on how well each of my people is doing on the job?
- Do I have accurate information on the results each of my people is producing?
- Do I have accurate information on how well my work unit is functioning?
- Do I have accurate information on the results my work unit is producing?

Answering yes to each of these questions is critical to truly knowing how well your operation is performing and what to do about it.

Practical Example—Supervising the Front Line at a Package-Handling Facility

The traditional role of the front-line supervisor at a large package-handling operation was one that relied solely on watching employees work and observing the time of departure of trucks from the dock. A new computer tracking system allowed supervisors to sit in the office and monitor employee package-handling performance by counting how many packages had been scanned into the system by each employee in fifteen-minute intervals. If an employee fell behind, that person was summoned to the office to explain and was generally reprimanded. Supervisors went from living on the dock and observing the operation in the heat and cold to living in a comfortable office behind a computer screen.

The problem was that the computer tracked only production and not quality-enhancing behaviors such as fixing a damaged customer order or seeking out a lost package or helping a coworker solve a problem. The supervisor monitored and measured only one facet of performance—individual performance data—and ignored both the behavioral and work-unit activity that affected performance. Morale suffered, quality suffered, and so did overall operational performance.

A new operations manager ordered the supervisors to come out of the office and split their time 40 percent at the computer and 60 percent in the operation to monitor and measure the complete picture. His instructions were noteworthy, "You can't lead and operate from behind a x@$!* computer, so get out on the dock and make it happen." His mandate brought much-needed balance to this operation, which had a very positive effect on overall performance.

■ **Practice 2: Motivate Employees to Create Ownership and Accountability**

IRREFUTABLE PERFORMANCE PRINCIPLE: When a manager motivates a workforce to create a sense of ownership and accountability for desired results, the job of getting results gets easier.

For a work unit to get desired results, it is imperative that the leader attempt to create an environment in which employees have a sense of ownership in the activity and output of the group. At the same time, there must be accountability for the achievement of desired levels of performance. In our interviews, although most managers spoke of motivating employees, more spoke of the importance of getting people to take ownership of their work, or helping people to feel like they are really part of something worthwhile, or helping people to increase their commitment. In the words of one manager, "When people take ownership of their work, you've made a quantum leap that goes beyond simply trying to motivate people. . . . Motivating people can be viewed as a gimmick or trick, but understanding how to make people feel like owners of their operation is an organizational lifestyle issue."

Thus, although a manager might use one or two motivational tools to try to increase an employee's short-term performance, the ultimate goal should be to develop and implement management practices that cause people to feel a sense of ownership and pride in their work. The difference might best be described as an employee working with you *as part of the team* as opposed to an employee working for you *because the organizational chart requires it.* When motivational techniques that have been proven to work individually are bundled together and implemented as a manager's modus operandi, good things happen. Conversely, when these issues are ignored, or are not taken seriously, or an organization's culture is set up to disenfranchise people, getting results becomes much more difficult and the workplace becomes more stressful.

The Importance of Stoking the Fire

To illustrate this point, read this actual resignation letter from a "broken employee" of a *Fortune* 500 organization, and look at the issues that caused him to separate himself from this enterprise.

> Dear Personnel,
> I want you to know why I am leaving after eleven years of hard work and dedication. I reached a point where I hated to come to work. It started to make me feel sick all the time and I realized life is too short to make myself sick for nothing. I worked hard but nobody ever noticed unless there was a problem and then everybody jumped all over me to protect their own ass. I worked in three different departments and it was always the same, we were disorganized and always fighting to keep on schedule and that gave me more stress than I needed. It didn't have to be that way but management would not listen to us. I had suggestions but my boss Mr. [Blank] told me to just work or that he'd look into it and nothin ever came from it. He made me feel dumb and at first I didn't like myself but then I didn't like him or his boss either. They both think their sh_t doesn't stink. Hey, why am

I being asked to give up pay and benefits when management makes lots of money? I read in the paper our president makes over a million bucks. What makes him so high and mighty? I don't have another job yet but I just had to get out of here or else go crazy, my work caused me big problems at home. Nobody will probably even read this letter because I am just a peon but if anybody does remember I never missed work, I did as I was told, and tried to help the company in my own way and was treated like a dog. I feel angry and don't know what else to say.

John [Surname]

A review of John's personnel file revealed that in eleven years, this employee did not miss one day's work. So was he motivated? For a while. But he sure didn't feel like an owner of the work that he was asked to perform. He was frustrated because he never got positive feedback and received too much negative feedback, because the operation was disorganized, and because management didn't listen to the workers about how to fix things and didn't follow up on commitments. The issue of fairness in compensation and benefits arose, and the worker was led to believe that he was simply a "peon" and "treated like a dog."

In short, this man was run off by the organization and management over key issues, issues that would be covered in any elementary discussion of motivation. Oh, by the way, this former employee was *never* late, *never* involved in an accident, and was described by his last supervisor as "extremely conscientious." And now he was gone. Was this organization serious about getting results? If actions speak louder than words, the answer is a resounding no! Yet given our experience, this organization and its managers are by no means the exception.

Here's an exercise to answer the question: *Do you use motivation as a tool to create ownership and accountability for desired performance?*

Find Out Now—Are You Turning Your People On or Off?

1. On a sheet of paper, make two columns. At the top of the first column, put the heading "Things That Turn My People On," and at the top of the second column "Things That Turn My People Off."
2. Complete each column.
3. Assess your lists. The odds are that, one way or another, your lists will address the key practices that are needed to create both ownership of and accountability for desired results (one way or another).

Motivation is most simply defined as an inner drive to satisfy a need. And the simplest explanation of motivation is one of the most powerful. *People are willing to expend effort when it satisfies some need that is important to them.* And since motivation is all about need-driven behavior, it is important for managers to understand how their actions and the culture of their organizations affect the ability of employees to satisfy their needs at work. While quotes and inspirational sayings abound on the topic of motivation—things like "When the going gets tough the tough get going"—we know that it is much easier for a manager to demotivate people than to motivate them. And when managers are asked to motivate their people or "fire them up" (stoke their fire), they can rather easily look manipulative and even shallow in their efforts because they are not thinking about the bigger picture of performance. Even proven motivational techniques break down when they are viewed as simply manipulative tools rather than part of a larger set of important and genuine managerial practices and actions.

Results-Oriented Managers Share Their Techniques

One of the great lessons that emerged from the interview portion of this research dealt with how results-oriented managers view motivation. Motivation is not simply a means to get people to pursue organizational goals; rather, it is a means to get people to buy in and take ownership of the organization's needs as well as their own. Managers shared a variety of specific practices in this regard. These practices fell into two categories: practices to increase ownership of performance and practices to create accountability for results.

Practices to Increase Ownership of Performance

- Develop a personal connection with each employee so that you know and understand that employee's strengths and weaknesses. Managers can encourage ownership by developing trust and maintaining a positive attitude with their employees.
- Clarify each employee's responsibility through effective delegation so that they all know what challenges they must meet and what work they must take ownership of.
- Ensure that people are properly trained and equipped to perform their work so they will feel prepared to succeed. Make it clear that you want *all* your people to be successful.
- Make sure that employees are empowered with the authority and information they need to make decisions that affect their performance.
- Involve employees in key practices that affect them—such as goal-setting, planning, and implementing change—so that they take ownership of decisions that affect them.
- Always listen to employees, and when problems emerge, encourage participation, new ideas, and ownership of solutions.
- Practice "open-book management" with employees in terms of sharing organizational and work-unit goals, plans, and performance feedback. In this way, your people see the bigger picture.
- Develop linkage between desired performance and rewards and incentives to demonstrate to people that there are good reasons to take ownership of their performance.

- Allow people an opportunity to grow and develop new skills and talents. Doing so causes people to be more committed to both the job and the organization.
- Celebrate success because people want to be part of a winning enterprise and because feeling successful makes it easier for people to come to work. Recognition for strong performance increases the desire for more good performance.

Practices to Create Accountability for Results

- When responsibilities and goals have been clarified, always establish standards of performance that should be challenging yet realistic enough to encourage people to hit the mark.
- Provide balanced, ongoing performance feedback for your people so that they know and have no doubt about how well they are performing.
- Provide ongoing coaching for your people on how to improve their performance and be very specific in doing so.
- Use the formal appraisal process as a strategic planning activity to review performance, identify ways to improve, and recognize and reinforce desired levels of performance.
- Deal with nonperformers who are damaging work-unit performance and morale by either implementing a corrective action program or setting the stage for the person's departure from the organization. To not do so is to send all the wrong messages to nonperformers and performers alike.

Now go back to your list from the exercise in this section, and see how many of these practices are things you identified and in which column. Even though managers had a great deal more to say about using motivational tools to create ownership and buy-in than they did about accountability alone, it is critical that *you* balance the two types of practices so that your people will know you are serious about getting short-term and long-term results.

Practical Example—Performance Diary of an MBA Student

Karen was a hard-driving, rising star in her organization. She had been promoted five times in ten years and had always been successful. Three years after her latest promotion, however, her department's performance was beginning to slip. From her staff of eleven professionals, she lost two key people to competitors. In an exit interview, one of her best performers said, "Karen, you are one of the smartest people I know about the financials, but you have no clue how to motivate the people in this department. . . . You talk down to us, you remind us that we work for you all the time, you set impossible goals, you give us a steady diet of criticism, you act like you listen to us but you don't follow up, and people really don't think you give a hoot about our careers, only yours. . . . I just wanted you to know that before I left. And by the way, this is not sour grapes because I think you are better than this."

Karen told us that hearing this was like "being punched in the stomach," and she felt completely caught off guard. During her whole career she had been promoted rapidly and had never gotten any specific negative feedback about her management style until now. Was this employee's assessment accurate? Were things really that bad? Were her people really working with her? Or for her? Karen needed to answer all these questions. The causes of her getting off track were serious and deep-rooted, but Karen did get back on track; we'll tell you how in Chapter Six.

■ Practice 3: Provide Ongoing Performance Feedback by Being a Good Coach

IRREFUTABLE PERFORMANCE PRINCIPLE: People cannot change their performance if they don't know there is a need to do so or if they don't know how to change.

Results-oriented managers must demonstrate skill at coaching in order to elevate the performance of their people. The word *coach* can have a variety of meanings, especially to those who played organized sports. Coach can mean "authoritarian" or "the order-giver," or "the person who calls the plays," or "disciplinarian." Becoming a real coach is a challenging proposition for most of us, especially when very few of us have coaches to help coach us to become good coaches.

Coaching—More Than Providing Feedback

In their best-selling book *Everyone's a Coach,* famous Miami Dolphins coach Don Shula and management authority Ken Blanchard make a very strong statement that there is much more to "real coaching" than simply providing feedback.[1] We agree. They make a strong case that for coaching to be effective, it must be grounded on a strong concern for people, values that include integrity and trust, and a system for achieving desired performance. All these factors are critical to the process. As Shula and Blanchard state, "the purpose of coaching is to improve both the person and their performance." They add, "Based on our research with managers, we identified five components of coaching, using the acronym COACH."

Concern for employees
Observation of behavior and performance
Alignment to adjust employee behavior and performance
Communication and feedback about performance to help shape behavior
Help to improve performance and make employees feel like owners

If coaching is defined as the process of providing performance feedback and specific input on how to improve employee performance, then our key COACH principles can make this process credible to an employee. Managers in our research frequently talked about the importance of a leader's credibility. Nowhere is this more important than in the role of a coach.

Here's an exercise to answer the question: *Do your people have a clear sense of their current level of performance and what they need to do to improve?*

Find Out Now—Are You a Real COACH?

1. On a piece of paper, write the names of each of your direct reports.
2. Beneath each name, write down two items: one positive piece of feedback that that person should receive about performance today and one suggestion for improving current performance that is critical to their success.
3. Then meet with each person and share this information with them in a genuine and sincere fashion and see what kind of reaction you get from them.
4. Analyze the range of employee responses to this coaching experience and evaluate the degree to which your coaching employed the five principles described in the acronym COACH.

It is our experience that most managers can be effective coaches when they take the time and make the effort to do so. But this time and effort can easily be consumed by activities of lesser importance. Consider implementing the COACH exercise on a regular basis to help your people know where they stand and that performance improvement is not only needed but also expected and is a top priority.

Anyone's performance can be seen as a function of the following equation:

$$Performance = Ability \times Motivation \times Support$$

It is a coach's job to monitor all three aspects and to understand the role of each in employee performance. If a leader is implementing the absolutes and key practices described up to this point, most of the key factors of this equation have been addressed. When employee performance is not where it needs to be, as an effective leader you must be proficient at diagnosing and responding appropriately to the cause of the performance deficiency. At the same time, you must reinforce and reward performance. Figure 4.3 is useful for understanding how to respond appropriately to employee performance.

When performance is not where it needs to be, the first questions the coach considers should target the issues of support. For example, do your employees have the equipment, tools, information, supplies, and authority or sanction they need to get the job done? Starting here is critical, because it tells your employees that you are willing to understand what is going on rather than assign blame. After reviewing the support issue, take time to assess the issues of ability and motivation. We've found that good coaches do this individually because people are like

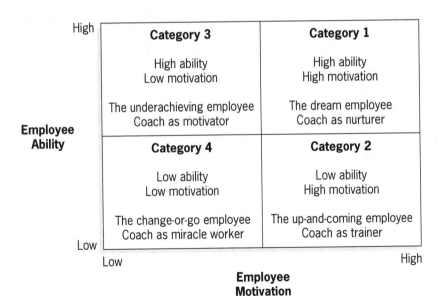

Figure 4.3. Employee Ability—Motivation Matrix

locks—each of them has a different key for unlocking personal performance.

Based on the motivation matrix given in Figure 4.3, here are the four categories of employees that emerged from our research.

- *Category 1: The Dream Employee.* Dream employees are highly skilled and highly motivated. They typically do what is expected, and then more. They are self-motivated, and they frequently look for additional work to do. It is easy to assume that these people do not need your attention or input, but don't take them for granted, because doing so can demotivate them. A good coach helps keep performance strong by identifying new and challenging job assignments, providing regular doses of praise and recognition, offering additional training and cross-training opportunities, granting additional authority, and letting such people know that they are appreciated. Here a coach's role is that of a nurturing leader.

- *Category 2: The Up-and-Coming Employee.* Up-and-coming employees can be a blessing to you as a coach because they are motivated and willing to work and learn. You help them by showing them how to improve their ability and skills. An effective coach observes and monitors employee performance and identifies the specific skills that need to be developed for improvement. The employee can then receive additional on-the-job training, formal training, and coaching to develop the requisite strength and ability. The intrinsic motivation of employees in this category means that they are likely to be willing students—people who *want* to learn. As coach, focus on the training issues associated with these employees' current needs to increase their performance by smoothing off any rough edges in terms of ability.

- *Category 3: The Underachieving Employee.* Underachieving employees frequently have the skill, experience, and ability to do great work when they want to, but their motivation (or lack thereof) tends to get in the way. Employees in this category frequently have negative attitudes, lack commitment, and do the bare minimum to get by. These employees are frequently labeled "underachievers" or "people on cruise control" because they fail to use their talents to the fullest. The use of both positive and negative consequences is generally required in responding to these employees to shape appropriate behaviors and performance. For these employees, your primary role is to motivate and increase their ownership of performance and their accountability for desired results. A good coach looks for ways to motivate the employee through the myriad of practices discussed thus far, and then helps the employee improve consistency and overall performance. In particular, look for ways to strengthen their connection with their work and workplace.

- *Category 4: The Change-or-Go Employee.* A worst-case scenario for a manager involves the change-or-go employees: those who lack the ability and skill to do the job *and* don't show any sign of being motivated to improve. These individuals might be bad hires, long-term survivors, or hangers-on, but in the end they are people who, for whatever reason, are not prepared or willing to perform. Change-or-go employees must do just that: change their performance or be asked to leave the enterprise because of the problems they cause and the damage they do to customers and fellow workers. Or, in the words of W. Edwards Deming, "Change the employee or change the employee." For these employees, a manager's role becomes that of miracle worker. It is necessary to simultaneously address the issues of both ability and motivation in a reasonable time frame—a tall order, at best. But we believe in miracles when people are confronted with the harsh consequences of nonperformance and failure to change. When performance standards are clearly established and communicated and are not being met, and the employee is not responding to attempts to improve, the coach's role shifts to that of a disciplinarian and documentor of poor performance to prepare for demotion or termination. Although this is often an unpleasant task, taking action demonstrates that performance standards matter to all concerned parties and can send a powerful motivational message.

Feedback—Nothing Is More Important!

It is critically important to maintain observation of both individual and work unit performance through effective interpersonal contact and MBWA[3]. At the same time, you must review performance data on a regular basis because to be an effective coach, you must know what is really going on around you. As a leader, develop the practice of providing your work unit with ongoing feedback about its performance against established goals and metrics. Help people keep score.[2]

At the same time, provide ongoing performance feedback to people on an individual level so that they know how well they are doing (and so they know that you know). We believe feedback is a lot like brushing your teeth. Is it better to brush your teeth three times a day for thirty consecutive days for a total of ninety minutes a month, or to brush once a month for ninety minutes? You decide. Performance feedback is the same way. It is optimal in small, regular doses that let people know how well they are doing in their quest to get results. The key point is that managers should provide regular feedback on any issues that are important to getting results.

Finally, as manager, sit down and discuss performance regularly with each of your people to make sure that they have the support they need and to get feedback from them on how things are going. Effective managers evaluate the ability and motivation of each of their people and then, with them, look for ways to support and improve performance. And while some managers will claim that they do not have time for this activity, it must be asked: What is more important than providing feedback and talking about how to improve performance? We believe the answer is quite clear, because failing to take time now means spending more time later dealing with the fallout of unnecessarily poor performance. We also recommend going through and assessing each of your people in the various coaching categories to think about what you can do to help them improve. Please make this assessment a priority.

Practical Example—Turnaround at a Manufacturing Plant

The managers of a manufacturing plant had developed the bad habit of providing performance feedback only when things were not going right, and their feedback was only negative. When things were going well, they feared that workers would slow down and sandbag the rest of the shift. When performance was down, workers would be assailed by management with pleas to "pick up the pace," "put the pedal to the metal," and "get the lead out"—often accompanied by threats of being laid off or terminated. The overall plant culture was extremely negative, and front-line managers did little to enhance worker performance. A union drive and poor productivity caused a new plant manager to be hired who implemented the following manifesto to the plant's management staff:

1. Every shift will have specific performance goals at the start of the shift and review the preceding day's performance.
2. At mid-shift the entire unit will receive feedback on their overall performance over the first four hours of the shift.
3. Each supervisor will meet with each of their direct reports at least five minutes per week to discuss their performance.
4. All supervisors will receive feedback on their shift and personal performance once every four weeks from their immediate superior. Failing to perform these tasks effectively means we are failing as leaders.
5. We will implement these practices faithfully and diligently because people have a right to know how well they are doing and how to improve their performance. Failing to perform these tasks effectively means we are failing as leaders.

These practices were implemented from the top of this facility down, with striking results in both productivity and morale. Feedback and coaching were tools that were very effective in changing people's be-havior and performance at this facility. And there is no reason that these practices cannot work for you with the same outcomes.

■ Practice 4: Remove Performance Barriers

> IRREFUTABLE PERFORMANCE PRINCIPLE: When man-agers consistently remove barriers to performance they make it easier for people to get their work done and achieve desired results.

The road to results is often filled with potholes that can easily stymie efforts to satisfy customers, increase revenues, and reduce costs. And although proactive managers alleviate many potential performance barriers by implementing the effective management practices we've been discussing, problems can and do occur. Per-formance barriers can be described as anything that prevents or damages an individual or work unit's ability to achieve desired results. And while some performance barriers are outside the con-trol of managers—the cost of capital, labor shortages, govern-ment-imposed paperwork, inflation, utility costs, currency exchange rates, and so on—we are concerned with performance barriers that managers can remove, but for whatever reason fail to do so.[3]

How Performance Barriers Arise

Without due care, managers can unknowingly erect perform-ance barriers around any of the issues discussed in this book. At the same time, when managers and employees try to get things done in rapidly changing, complex organizational systems, per-formance barriers can and do pop up.

To illustrate, a vice president of bank operations recently shared a list of performance barriers with us that we believe is illustrative of what all managers are up against in the twenty-first century:

- Personnel policies are not conducive to retaining top employees.
- Advanced technology creates problems in terms of bringing a new, real-time information system on-line in a timely fashion.
- Ineffective front-line managers oversee customer service reps in several key locations.
- Corporate and branch banks fail to communicate and cooperate over lending procedures.
- Retail and commercial lending managers compete internally.
- Teller turnover and lack of retention practices are reaching critical points at several locations.
- Communication has broken down within several key branches.
- The employee handbook and policies are outdated.
- Current development programs for front-line managers are ineffective.

As managers, we know that we must be effective problem solvers and decision makers, but we must first solve the most pressing problems that affect our results. The key is to systematically identify and remove performance barriers in a timely fashion, yet with a sense of urgency. It is this quality that enables effective leaders to improve performance in the long run.

Here's an exercise to answer the question: *Do I work to systematically identify and remove performance barriers that get in the way of getting desired results?*

Find Out Now—Are You a Performance Barrier Buster?

1. Get your staff together and ask each of them to individually identify one on-the-job problem that creates a barrier they would like to see resolved to improve performance.

2. Compile a master list of all the problems that are identified, and ask the group to select the problem whose resolution would do the most to improve performance. (Larger groups can be subdivided into smaller groups, and each can identify different problems to address.)

3. Ask each group to develop solutions and a plan of action to solve the problem. Give each group adequate time to work out a solution, and then ask each group to present their findings.

4. Ask yourself these questions:

   Was I surprised by any of the problems that were identified?

   Did I agree with the group on the problem that they considered to be most important to improving performance?

   Does their plan of action really remove the performance barrier?

   Am I willing to implement this plan of action?

This exercise typically demonstrates how close a manager is to the performance needs of the work unit and how willing the manager is to listen and serve the needs of the people in removing performance barriers. What would happen to work-unit performance if this exercise in "barrier busting" became a way of organizational life? Ownership of the work would go up, and systems, policies, procedures, and practices would be aligned to improve work-unit performance. Achieving this happy result requires that the manager and the staff develop prowess in the problem-solving and decision-making process.

Busting the Performance Barrier

When it comes to removing performance barriers, the following guidelines emerged from our study—described by managers who also stated that although these steps are quite common they are frequently not applied in the heat of battle. These guidelines relate heavily to the process for removing performance barriers sketched in Figure 4.4.

To expand on the figure, here are the steps in more detail:

1. Identify the most urgent performance barriers to attack. That is, pick out the ones that will have the greatest impact on performance.
2. Make sure that you properly define the problem, and use data (when available) to identify the key variables of concern.

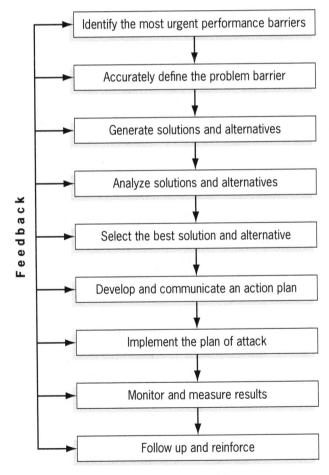

Figure 4.4. The Problem-Solving Barrier-Busting Model

3. Generate solutions and alternatives by getting "outside the box" and freely thinking about how to remove this particular barrier.

4. Analyze your options, using any and all appropriate data, to truly understand how each solution will affect the operation in both the short and long term and both positively and negatively.

5. Select the best option given the constraints of the situation, again using all data and decision-making tools available. Remember that as a leader you must balance consensus building with the need for timely action and effective leadership.

6. Develop an action plan that addresses the who, what, where, when, how, and why issues of your initiative to remove the barrier. Communicate the plan to all concerned and involved parties.

7. Implement the plan of attack by physically changing procedures, systems, policies, behaviors, and the like as needed to support this change. Remember that most changes fail when the people involved are not included in the process and don't alter their behavior or work habits when a decision is made.

8. Monitor and measure the impact and results of the change to see if it is having the desired effect in removing the performance barrier.

9. As the barrier to performance comes down, continue to monitor and reinforce desired behaviors and outcomes to ensure a lasting change.

Performance barrier busting can be done by you alone as a manager, by a problem-solving team of employees, or by a cross-functional team. The model doesn't change, but the process does, as you assert leadership and decide how to best approach and remove the barrier. Managers frequently lose credibility and burn up resources when they use teams inappropriately to attack barriers and problems that they should be taking on by themselves.

Removing performance barriers can be an easy thing—like finding a new service contractor to keep your photocopier in operation—or as complex as ironing out the bugs in a sophisticated manufacturing process. The important point is that, as leader, you take the initiative to identify the barriers and fix them, either by yourself or with the aid of concerned parties. Your goal needs to be to make it easier for people to get their work done. And if you systematically engage your people in the process of barrier busting, you will be building ownership of the solution. The advantage of managing by walking around, having interpersonal contact with your people, and keeping your eye on your performance scorecard is that you'll know when problems pop up. When a manager fails to fix things and lets little problems fester, bigger problems are on the horizon. Remember that small problems are like shoots of crabgrass that can quickly grow and spread to engulf your organizational turf and ruin your best efforts to get results. And when substantive and objective problems go unresolved, they almost always degenerate into interpersonal or even group conflict, which is a whole other potential barrier to performance. In the end, removing performance barriers builds a leader's credibility and makes it easier for people to do their work.

Practical Example—A Regional Trucking Company Develops an Action Plan

A regional trucking company had thirty terminals located in the southern United States. The garage operations at each of these facilities were responsible for ensuring that each tractor-trailer rig that left the facility was ready to "hit the road." The problem was that the work done at each garage was charged against the budget for that facility. So when budgets got tight, front-line supervisors were tempted (and often gave in to their temptation) to send trucks on the road that actually needed repairs, hoping and praying that they would make it to the next facility before they had any serious problems. The budgeting and cost-allocation system was causing this problem, and everyone knew it except top management, who considered the current system to be working effectively. Garage managers knew it caused problems but the policy was viewed as a sacred cow by top management, so no one was willing to take the problem on. Front-line supervisors lost all credibility with the workforce—including the drivers—for complying with this policy, and there were serious safety concerns. After a number of problems, a new front-line supervisor formed a safety team on his own and studied the problem. He developed an action plan, which he submitted to the garage manager, copying the VP of Maintenance and the CEO. After a major uproar and a site visit with top executives, the young front-line supervisor and his team who did the right thing had the system changed to encourage the right actions. The performance barrier was removed and the organization was better off, because of the courage and actions of one person. The young supervisor who took a chance won the respect of many people and a promotion in the end.

CHAPTER SUMMARY

It is important to remember that "stoking the fire" of performance is an absolute because many of today's employees don't necessarily come to work all fired up the way their parents and grandparents were in the past. Instead they frequently look to their boss and organization to light their fire for performance. Therefore, when managers take appropriate steps to create a climate for achievement and stoke the fire of performance, the workplace becomes more conducive to high performance and getting desired results. Knowing what is really going on around you, motivating your people to create ownership and accountability, providing ongoing feedback and coaching, and removing performance barriers are all critical practices necessary to improve long-term performance. When a manager does these practices well, both individual and workforce performance improve. Conversely, when managers fail to take these processes seriously, employees can easily conclude that they are not serious about getting results. As one manager from this study told us, "In today's workplace, if you don't take extreme care in your attempt to turn your people on there is a good chance that you might be turning them off—and then everybody loses." This is a thought worth remembering!

Absolute #4

Build Bridges on the Road to Results: Nurture Relationships with People

Throughout our exploration of how managers go about getting results, there is an underlying theme of the importance of tapping into people power, which reminds us of a story from the Great Depression. A farmer in Texas had a large spread that drought had turned into a dust bowl. The bank was preparing to foreclose on the property, when the farmer decided to walk his land one last time, seeking wisdom about what to do. As the farmer walked, he came to a rise, and when he looked down he noticed a black puddle on the ground. This puddle turned out to be oil. The pressure from beneath the surface had pushed the hidden "black gold" to a place where it could now be seen. As it turned out, the farmer had been walking right on top of a huge resource that had the potential to greatly change his life. But up to this point that resource had been unknown and untapped. The oil field was huge, and the farmer went on to become a successful oilman. But first he had to develop techniques to tap into the oil systematically and put it to use.

So it is with people (who are often called *resources*) in the workplace. Sometimes people power pushes itself to the surface on its own. An employee, for instance, demonstrates uncommon customer service or solves a troubling production problem single-handedly, or simply devises a better way of doing things without being asked. Other times managers have to drill through thick bedrock to tap into their employees' full energy potential. In both situations, the difference between *being busy* and *getting results* is frequently the strength and quality of the bridges that a manager builds with people.

A recent book by Dave Ulrich, Jack Zenger, and Norm Smallwood, *Results-Based Leadership,* made it clear that the ability of a manager to "relate to people" and "create an environment that made people feel like part of a team" is critical to employee retention, motivation, and performance.[1] These views greatly support our findings: A manager must become adroit at "bridge-building" relationships—with superiors, peers, employees, and other parties critical to getting things done. Stated differently, there is a big difference between having people who work for you because they *have to* and people who work with you because they *want to.*

Have you ever had a boss you simply didn't connect with and with whom you really never developed an effective working relationship? How did this affect your performance, attitude, and behavior? How about a peer? Truth be known, results-oriented managers take great care in developing effective working relationships, a fact often overlooked in our fast-paced, productivity-driven workplace.

Quiet! Here He Comes!

Tom was a marketing director with a global agriculture business. He had high energy, high standards, and great marketing acumen. He was intelligent, motivated, and terrific with customers. There was just one serious problem with Tom's approach to business: he couldn't get the people who worked around him to trust him. They viewed him as self-serving, unable to build cooperation between his department members, quick to pounce on anyone whose performance wasn't meeting goals, and prone to losing his temper. He had a tendency to talk down to his people, failed to keep people informed, and was for all intents and purposes "unapproachable" unless he needed something. After he'd been on the job for a year, people tended to avoid him at all costs, and there was a common refrain as he walked the halls: "Quiet! Here he comes!" as people would disperse to avoid any contact with him. In a nutshell, the people in the marketing department "went turtle in the shell" because of his inability to connect with his large staff. As a result, performance suffered.

Tom was very talented and had all the skills necessary to be an excellent manager—that is, all the skills but one, the ability to build bridges with *all* the people he needed to achieve high levels of performance. He was capable of building bridges—after all, customers loved him. His own staff, however, was simply working for him rather than working with him because of his attitude and the way he treated them. The critical components of respect, trust, and cooperation were missing, and by failing to treat those around him properly, he burned bridges in ways that damaged his own career and performance as well as those of his people.

To get better results these days, managers must build bridges by following four key practices: forging effective 360-degree working relationships, demonstrating trustworthy leadership, practicing all facets of effective communication, and fostering teamwork and cooperation. These four practices (given in Figure 5.1) are critical for managers to build the people power necessary to support performance in bridging the gap between current

Performance

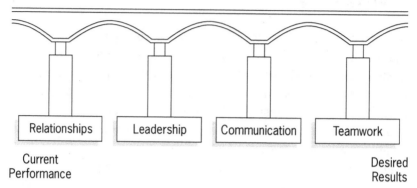

Figure 5.1. Building the Bridge to Results

performance and desired results and to implement the twelve management practices discussed in preceding chapters.

To illuminate the importance of effective bridge building in your quest for better results, we can do no better than share the following statement from the general manager of a high-tech company:

> I remember one of my first bosses said something to me that has stayed with me my whole career. He told me my behavior as a manager would either be building bridges with the people I need to get things done or burning bridges with the same people. It is sobering to think that my behavior can either fire people up or flame people off. So I am very careful about how to interact with my people because I can ill afford to set a lot of bridges on fire and still enjoy coming to work and getting things done.

■ Practice 1: Forge Effective 360-degree Working Relationships

IRREFUTABLE PERFORMANCE PRINCIPLE: Results-oriented managers foster effective 360-degree working relationships with all people who are important to getting results, and they continually work to keep these relationships viable.

One of the basic tenets of modern organizations is the concept of *systems thinking*. According to this view, organizations are complex systems made up of subsystems. Managers must understand the interactions and interdependencies of each component part. A change in one part of a complex system affects other parts, so when a manager wants to make a change in an operation, it will most likely require the assistance of another part of the enterprise, which may in turn affect yet another part of the enterprise. For example, any manager wanting to improve quality will most likely need the assistance of the information technology people, the engineering department, the human resources manager, and quite possibly the training department, which in turn affects other departments involved.

And while discussions of systems can be tedious, the real issue here is that complex organizational systems are really made up of people—people with different personalities, needs, and agendas—who ultimately need each other to get things done (although they don't always act like it). Operating in complex systems requires tremendous people skills to forge effective working relationships. It has always been one of our basic contentions that most people are not sufficiently prepared to develop effective working relationships because of a failure on the part of the formal education systems. We are taught a great deal about the Three R's of education—*reading, riting,* and *rithmetic*—but we receive surprisingly little formal training on the fourth R—*relating to people.* To illustrate the point, most college programs in business administration, engineering, and computer science will probably have one course in interpersonal communication or speech and maybe an elective in organizational behavior. But that is it. Less than 5 percent of the total coursework is designed to prepare people to understand how to work together effectively.

Yet these same programs will pile on the calculus, statistics, computer programming, and analytical courses to ensure the technical competency of their graduates. We see the same process repeating itself at the graduate level of education. Although quantitative skills are important to success, they are insufficient alone in preparing a person for the workplace. The root cause of most business problems these days is the inability of people to get together and work together. The Old Testament contains an account of how Samson killed ten thousand Philistines with the jawbone of an ass. We believe that tens of thousands of working relationships are destroyed each and every day with the exact same weapon!

In our survey, when managers made it clear that developing effective working relationships was critical to getting results, we probed deeply during interviews to learn more about what managers meant by this. There was a very simple consensus: No one wants to work for or with someone that they consider to be a jerk! We hope that this statement does not offend the sensibilities of the reader but there is no gentle or easy way to say it. Jerkish behaviors and attitudes that destroy managerial effectiveness include berating people in public, taking all credit for success and no blame for failures, treating people with disrespect and contempt, being a con artist and manipulator, lying and lacking integrity, being "always right" and argumentative, talking down to people and never listening, rumor mongering and being a gossip, behaving inconsistently and erratically, and displaying a "me-first" approach to everything. All these things have one thing in common: they flame people off instead of firing people up.

Results-oriented managers identify and foster effective working relationships up, down, and sideways that are based on honesty, mutual dependency, and mutual support. They know there is a cost associated with arrogance, contempt, communication breakdowns, posturing, politicking, lying, power trips, and winning at someone else's expense. They take great care to develop effective 360-degree working relationships with the people they need to get the work done. In the words of one manager, "As our organization flattens, I find myself having to develop better relationships with people than in the past because my direct authority over people is going down and my needs from other people around here are going up. . . . And good working relationships don't just happen!"

Here's an exercise to answer the following question: *Do I have effective working relationships with* all *of the people I need to get my work done?*

Find Out Now—Are Your Working Relationships Working?

1. On a sheet of paper, list by name all of the people you count on to get the results you desire.
2. Then prioritize your list of names in order of importance for getting results.
3. Rate the quality of each of these working relationships using the scale in Worksheet 5.1.
4. Now identify the working relationships that are currently damaging performance and are in need of attention. Walk through the following set of questions to analyze how to improve each of these relationships—whether with your boss, a peer, an employee, or a member of another department:

   What do I need from this person that I am not getting?

   What do they need from me that I am not providing?

   What is the real problem here?

   How is this problem damaging our performance?

   What can I do to make this relationship more effective?

   What do we need to do together to make this relationship more effective?

Without effective working relationships in all directions it becomes more difficult than need be to improve performance and get things done.

■ Worksheet 5.1. Relationship Review ■			
	Performance Damaging		Performance Enhancing	

Employee Name	Broken Working Relationship	Strained Working Relationship	Positive Working Relationship	Highly Effective Working Relationship
	☐	☐	☐	☐
	☐	☐	☐	☐
	☐	☐	☐	☐
	☐	☐	☐	☐
	☐	☐	☐	☐

What Makes an Effective Working Relationship?

Managers in our study described many of the attributes of effective working relationships that are worth noting. Here is a list we compiled:

- Expectations and performance needs are clearly defined.
- Communication and personal exchanges are two-way.
- The parties have mutual respect and trust.
- The parties have a shared sense of responsibility to each other for outcomes.
- The parties display common courtesy and appropriate social behavior.
- The parties have a personal interest in each other and show a "human touch."
- Social exchanges are not contingent on performance needs alone.
- Each party has empathy for the other's needs and goals.

- The parties engage in ongoing joint problem-solving and conflict-resolution activities.
- The parties display lightheartedness, fun, and minimal sarcasm and negative attitudes.

This list is not earth shattering, but if these practices were to become a bigger part of organizational life, things would be more productive and people would be less likely to leave organizations for the wrong reasons. In the words of our managers, "Good working relationships don't just happen; they require time, effort, and focus."

Daniel Goleman, author of *Working with Emotional Intelligence*, makes an exceedingly strong case for the importance of managers placing more focus on working relationships within the workplace.[2] *Emotional intelligence* is described as people's ability to manage themselves and their relationships effectively. It is driven by four fundamental capabilities: self-awareness, self-management, social awareness, and social skill. A critical finding from a random sample of 3,871 managers selected from a global database of twenty thousand executives indicated that managers' effectiveness in any given business situation was influenced by their ability to manage themselves and critical working relationships effectively. This required managers to be sufficiently in touch with themselves to adapt their style and their approach to interactions and leadership to the demands of any given situation. The conclusion here is that results-oriented managers adapt to make needed working relationships work rather than assuming the other party will change to meet their needs.

This can be a real challenge for anyone. In today's pressure-packed organizations it is easy for a manager to dominate a relationship or conversation, to take more than is given, to ignore common courtesy, to be abrupt and possibly engage in the destructive practice of sarcasm or "dark humor" as a way of life.

Remember, though, that nobody wants to work for or with someone who doesn't know how to work with people (that is, who is a jerk). There is a cost associated with not being able to work with others, which can frequently manifest itself in reduced performance.

When a Working Relationship Isn't Working

If a working relationship is not working and it is getting in the way of performance, as a results-oriented manager you would respond to this situation as you would any other performance problem—analyze the situation, identify the problem, select an appropriate action, and implement the change. Although relationships can be complex, they require the same type of thinking and attention as other things do when they are broken, strained, and dysfunctional. Do not assume that time alone will heal or fix problems that prevent people from working together.

Occasionally, people who need each other to get things done simply don't like each other. Or they get off to a bad start that is the beginning of something that only gets uglier. Egos, personality clashes, bad attitudes, and a lack of concern for others can be at the base of highly emotional situations.

More often, though, strained working relationships evolve over disagreements, problems, or frustrations concerning issues of substance that never get discussed or resolved. Disagreements over expectations, facts, policies, deadlines, job assignments, goals, plans, resource allocations, procedures, performance standards, and intended meanings can all damage working relationships and create huge performance barriers. If these substantive issues are left to fester, they will degenerate into emotional conflicts that are infinitely more difficult to resolve.

Improving working relationships is not a warm, fuzzy thing. Instead, it focuses on identifying and resolving the problems that prevent optimal performance. Note that by our actions alone we can strengthen and improve many working relationships—by communicating better, offering more feedback, taking a more personal interest in people, and keeping our part of every bargain (and *our word*). The good news here is that when results-oriented managers internalize the absolutes from this research and make it part of their mode of operation, they are proactively improving the quality of many working relationships (with their boss and employees) from the start. The problem occurs when managers fail to make relationships a priority and fail to take stock of their own skills and abilities as they pertain to building good relationships. When managers have ego problems, are unapproachable, have a short fuse, cannot be trusted, or are generally abrasive to people around them and they don't know or care about it, long-term performance is significantly compromised. There is no substitute for regularly assessing the quality and effectiveness of working relations as you have just done in the preceding exercise. By keeping relationships viable a manager will find it easier to make work more productive and less stressful.

Practical Example—
Secrets of a "People-Person" Career Executive

The best results-oriented manager we know is also one of the best "people persons" we know. John is a career executive who is very performance-driven, but he has a unique characteristic. During his long career as a troubleshooter for six large corporations, he has made it a policy to nail down early on exactly what he is being paid to achieve. He then studies the organization, getting to know everyone who is important to getting things done. He cares about people, and he believes relationships must be mutually beneficial. He's on a first-name basis with everyone in the organization in short order—from the president to the maintenance man—and he uses voluminous amounts of thank-you, birthday, and anniversary cards to recognize others for their contributions.

He operates with the simple belief that gossip has no place in leadership and that if people do not trust him he has lost twice: professionally and personally. His technical skills are sharply honed, but it's his ability to build a network of effective working relationships that is the envy of many other managers. His secret: "You've got to have a passion to work with others, constantly improve your own interpersonal skills, and, maybe most important, budget time each and every week to have contact with people all around you to listen, observe, and exchange information. *Just like a bank—I can't take out of the bank what I haven't put in.*"

■ Practice 2: Demonstrate Leadership Worthy of Trust

IRREFUTABLE PERFORMANCE PRINCIPLE: There is no substitute for competency and character in developing trustworthy leadership that fosters long-term success.

Leadership has been and continues to be one of the most studied, analyzed, discussed, and written-about topics in the field of management. Leadership is frequently described as *the ability to influence and inspire people toward the achievement of goals.* And although leadership is a critical component of the management process, it is not the same thing as management. So how do managers get people to follow their lead? This is an important question to answer because if you are in a management position and no one is following you then you are really just taking a walk by yourself, which raises another critical question. Is your organization willing to pay you to just take a walk? Highly doubtful these days!

Here's an exercise to answer the following question: *As a manager do I lead by example and demonstrate competency and character on a consistent basis?* To find out whether you give your people sufficient reasons to follow you, put yourself in the position of being one of your own employees and then go through the following steps.

Find Out Now—Why Would I Follow You?

1. Write down this question: *Why should I follow you?*
2. Write five responses.
3. Analyze your list and consider these questions:

   What does the list look like?

   Was it difficult to come up with?

   Would your employees agree?

Having posed this question to literally thousands of managers, the responses ran the gamut. Here are some of the more representative ones.

> *You would want to follow me as a leader because . . .*
>
> You'll always know where you stand.
>
> I'll help you reach your goals.
>
> I'll keep you in the loop.
>
> We'll get things done together.
>
> I'll teach you everything I know.
>
> I'll always listen to you.
>
> I'll get you the resources you need to get the job done.
>
> I'll try to make work fun.
>
> I know where we are going and how to get there.
>
> You need me to be successful.
>
> I can help your career.
>
> I reward good performance.
>
> My word is golden.

The set of responses just given represents something that emerged in our research but that is often overlooked in discussions of leadership. Employees will follow a manager's lead when two critical leadership components are present: *competency* and *character.*

The Importance of Competency and Character

Leadership *competency* can be described as the ability leaders have to perform the various functions of their job that are most critical to facilitating the performance of the followers. That is to say, leaders must perform the right functions, and they must perform these functions well to best support employee performance. A leader's *character* can be described as personal "moral makeup" as it pertains to integrity, honesty, sound judgment, self-discipline, managerial courage, and respect for others.

Both questionnaire and interview data constantly told the story of the importance of "moral leadership," "treating people with dignity," integrity," "value-based decision making," and "high ethical standards" coupled with leadership competency as being the key to followers' trusting their leaders. This trust factor makes it easier for an employee to follow a manager's lead. In his best-selling book *Principle-Centered Leadership*, Stephen Covey makes a simple observation: "If I try to use manipulative strategies and tactics to get other people to do what I want— while my character is flawed or my competency is questionable—then I cannot be successful over time. Rhetoric and good intentions aside, if there is little or no trust, there is no foundation for permanent success."[3]

Without the trust of followers, the ability of a manager to tap into and unleash people power is greatly diminished. That is why the key practice here is the manager's ability to demonstrate leadership that is worthy of employees' trust (which will drive their willingness to follow). This concept can be visualized as in Figure 5.2.

As shown in the figure, if a leader is competent to lead but lacks moral character, employee trust in the leader will not be strong. Employees will have feelings of uncertainty, doubt, and even fear. These factors diminish employees' willingness to fol-

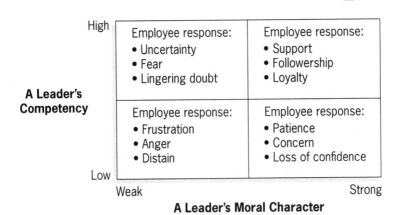

Figure 5.2. Employee Response to Leader Trust

low the leader. Conversely, if a leader lacks the skills necessary to lead but is a person of high moral character, then the employees will "buy time for themselves" while their manager acquires the necessary skills because people will typically want this person to succeed (so a level of patience will emerge). If skill development (competency) is not forthcoming, concerns over their leader's fitness for command will emerge. This concern will be followed by a loss of confidence, as the "moral manager" is damaging performance.

When a leader lacks both competency and character, employees will experience frustration, anger, and eventually disdain for both the individual and the people who placed this person in this position. In all three of these scenarios the employees' level of trust in the leader is called into question, with unfortunate outcomes. Modern employees want both competency and character in the leader who is affecting their livelihood.

The optimal situation is one in which employees trust both the professional competency of their leaders and their character. The trust that develops increases their willingness not only to follow but also to support and demonstrate loyalty on behalf of the manager in question, which truly helps set the table for increased performance.

How Do You Develop Competency and Character?

In developing your trustworthiness as a leader, two things become pertinent. First, your people will judge your competency to lead based on your ability to meet the needs they have that pertain to getting their work done. In Chapter Two we talked about the importance of a manager's aligning behavior and actions with the needs of employees and developing a performance script. To create followers, as a leader you must effectively perform the functions that facilitate the performance of your followers, and you must do this well. Ask yourself the following questions:

- Do you have the skills your job requires?
- Are you using your skills to perform the functions needed by your people to get their work done?
- Is your leadership style meeting the needs of individual employees?

Second, you must be a person of character as demonstrated by your integrity and honesty with the people around you. A leader whose behavior is "beyond reproach," whose "word is golden," and who can be "trusted with anything" is a leader whose people will go the extra mile to get things done. Ask yourself the following questions:

- Is your word golden?
- Do you treat everyone with dignity and respect?
- Do you treat people as you would like to be treated?
- Can your employees trust you "with anything"?

There is no substitute for either of these leadership components in the quest for long-term success. Our willingness to work hard and go the extra mile for trustworthy leaders begins as youngsters, as evidenced by this "end of the year letter" written by a fourth-grade student to his teacher:

Dear Ms. Breese,
Thanks for being my teacher this year because I learned a lot. You sure can teach. You are the best teacher I ever had. You made us work hard and we did lots of homework but that was OK. You listened to me and told me when I did good. You even came to school when you were sick. You played with us on the playground and threw a hardball too. You didn't have bad breath like our teacher last year and you told good stories in class too. Thanks for taking care of me when I threw up in class and cleaning up my vomit. Mom told me that I work hard for you because I respect you because you respect us. I am not always sure what respect means but I do know I learned lots from you, I did my best, you are my friend, and we had a great class. I hope you are my teacher again someday soon. I will never forget you even when I am in the fifth grade.

God Bless You
Tommy

This teacher was able to get extra effort from her students because she knew "how to teach" (competency) and—equally important—because she demonstrated personal character and concern for her students. She listened, gave positive feedback, met the students on their turf (the playground), made class interesting, performed undesirable tasks (cleanup), and she did not have bad breath. The end result of this respect was respect returned and a willingness to work hard to learn and do one's best. This is a great lesson in leadership worthy of trust, one that can benefit all who emulate it.

Practical Example—
Improving Communication in a Finance Department

Sue took over the finance department of a large service organization after what she later learned was a "three-year reign of maleficence" by her predecessor. Sue had always been a very hands-on manager—close to her people and yet capable of making difficult decisions. During her first few weeks on the job, she realized that her staff were "icy in interpersonal exchanges," "sugar-coating" problems, and summarily keeping their distance from her. This was a source of tension for Sue because she couldn't seem to connect with people and so began doubting her abilities. She made sure that she was doing whatever she could to help her people get their work done. She clarified expectations, provided ongoing feedback, openly shared operating information, identified and helped solve some problems that were damaging performance, and got her people involved in the planning process. Ever so slowly, individuals began to open up to her. Communication improved, as did the overall climate of the department. But it was moving much more slowly than Sue would have liked. One day one of Sue's senior analysts came to her office with a problem and at the end of the meeting shared an observation.

"Sue, when you got here this department was like a dog that had been kicked one too many times. It was everyone for themselves, and nobody trusted anybody because of our previous manager. We had been conditioned by his cutthroat style of management to be afraid and not trust him or anyone else around here. He'd yell about getting the work done on time and the lack of quality and on and on, but he did nothing to really help us do our work. To be honest, we hated him. You've felt some of those bad feelings since you arrived, even though you've done a great job. It has taken a while for us to learn to trust you, but we now know that we can. Thanks for personally helping me get back on track and for treating us with the respect that we needed. You can count on us in the future because you've earned our respect."

Sue greatly appreciated the feedback, but was sobered by the realization that there was no quick fix in earning the trust of her people.

■ **Practice 3: Establish Open, Ongoing,
and Focused Two-Way Communication**

> IRREFUTABLE PERFORMANCE PRINCIPLE: A manager's
> ability to meet people's communication needs is critically im-
> portant to success and requires both skill and a systematic
> process.

Managers in this study identified five burning communication
needs that people have in these times of rapid change, restructuring, and pressure for improved performance:

- To have the information they need to do their work effi-
  ciently and effectively
- To feel informed about the things taking place in the organization as a whole that might affect their future
- To have a vehicle through which their voice can be heard
- To have confidence and trust in the people responsible for
  these three processes
- To have an overall communication process that is ongoing
  and systematic rather than pell-mell and crisis driven

These communication needs must be met if leaders are
truly going to lead their people to better performance. This practice requires open, ongoing, and focused two-way communication, which are the hallmarks of communicating for results and
having competency and character as a leader. Without this foundation, attempts at communicating can simply become an informational exchange, or worse yet, just noise!

We often ask employees, "If you could improve one thing
in this organization, what would it be?" In most organizations,
communication is the most frequent response from employees
to this question. This tends to frustrate managers—who tend to

respond with plaints like, "What kinds of information do people want that they are not already getting?" This response is natural, but it misses the real point. Communicating is not simply about sharing information. Organizations have never had more vehicles to use for communicating, and yet ask yourself a very simple question: Are we communicating more or less effectively than we did in the past? Most people will respond "less effectively," for several reasons:

- We are moving very fast, which can damage our ability to communicate effectively.
- We are all wrestling with voluminous amounts of data and information, which can cause overload.
- We have often dumbed down our definition of *communication* to mean simply sharing information and data, which leaves out the context and whether anyone understood the message.

These trends can damage a manager's ability to meet the five basic communication needs. While cell phones, pagers, Palm Pilots, fax machines, informational Web sites, and e-mail afford us the opportunity to share and disseminate copious amounts of information, a results-oriented manager will not mistake these *tools* for the effective communication that people want and need. The real goals of effective communication ought to be twofold: to understand others and what is really going on and to be understood and trusted. None of the absolutes discussed in the book can be implemented and practiced effectively without achieving these two overarching goals.

What Effective Communication Is

Effective communication is the glue that holds together effective working relationships, leadership that encourages trust, meaningful coaching, motivation that creates ownership and accountability and all forms of employee involvement and participation.

Or in the words of one executive, "If I'm not communicating effectively with my people, then I am probably miscommunicating, which can only mean trouble ahead." Thus effective communication for a results-oriented manager focuses on meeting the communication needs of the people around them rather than simply sharing information that they consider to be important.

Here's an exercise to answer the following question: *Do I communicate with all of the people I need to reach so as to satisfy their communication needs and get results?*

Find Out Now—Are You Really Communicating?

1. Ask yourself each of the questions in Worksheet 5.2 to assess the degree to which you are meeting the communication needs of the people you need to get results.
2. Now ask yourself this question: If you were arrested for being a poor communicator, would there be enough evidence at the trial for your acquittal?

One executive in our study said, "I strongly believe that most managers can be great communicators if they want to. . . . The catch is getting them to want to when they are moving a hundred miles per hour, with a to-do list as long as your arm. . . . If managers' lives depended on making sure their people were in the loop and knew what was really going on, they'd do it. . . . Well, it's time to realize that our professional lives and livelihood do depend on that very thing." Although the choice of words might seem dramatic, when managers do not practice effective communication they are endangering their future.

Stop for a moment and think of all the opportunities you have to communicate with your people in informal and formal settings. The list is long:

- One-on-one in informal daily contact
- One-on-one in formal settings like performance reviews and coaching sessions

■ Worksheet 5.2. Communications Assessment ■				
To What Extent Do I . . .	Rarely	Sometimes	Usually	Always
1. Provide complete information people need to get their work done?	☐	☐	☐	☐
2. Provide information that people need to feel informed about what is happening in the organization as a whole?	☐	☐	☐	☐
3. Provide effective vehicles for people's inputs and concerns to be heard?	☐	☐	☐	☐
4. Foster credibility and trust in the communication process?	☐	☐	☐	☐
5. Provide opportunities to understand and be understood on an ongoing and systemic basis?	☐	☐	☐	☐

- Staff meetings
- Formal presentations and discussions
- E-mail
- Telephone conversations
- Written interpersonal correspondence
- Operating system reports
- Group planning and problem-solving meetings
- Posting of information either physically or electronically

The questions to ask are these: Does the vehicle of communication match the needs of the employee? Is the method of communication effective in meeting employee needs? Remember, employees want information to do their work, to feel informed, and to have a voice—and they want it from a source they trust in a systematic fashion.

Meet the Communication Needs of Your People

If your goal is to understand and know what is going on around you and to be understood and trusted, you need a focused and systematic communication system that meets the communication needs of your people. Take the time to develop one if you haven't already done so. Based on the input of managers in this study, we can confidently assert that people need the right information, at the right time, at the right place, in the right form, from the right person. Providing too little (or too much) information, at the wrong time, at the wrong place, in the wrong form, from the wrong person only creates more problems for a manager and wastes time and energy. *Systematic communication* means that processes are developed to help people understand and be understood on the issues that are most important for them to get their work done and to know what is going on around them.

Input from managers in this study makes it clear that different levels of management have different communication demands placed on them, but all managers are well served by developing a focused and systematic communication system that addresses each of the following five areas:

- *Needs.* What specific informational needs do people have to be able to function effectively?

  Job-Related

  Organization-Related
- *Importance.* Is the information to be communicated "need to know" or just nice to know?
- *Vehicle.* What vehicles are most appropriate for communicating in a particular situation to meet people's needs?

- *Frequency.* How often do we need to communicate on any particular issue?
- *Effectiveness.* How can we ensure that people's communication needs are actually being met?

The answers to each of these questions can help you develop a systematic approach that allows you and your people to be understood and to understand each other and what is really going on around them. In addition, all managers should communicate as much as possible using the *KISS principle:* Keep It Short (and) Simple. This reminds us to stay focused and to communicate in a fashion that helps get the message out and understood.

Practical Example—
One Manager's Communication System

A new general manager took over a complex division of a large international steel manufacturing organization. His nine direct reports were all strong, capable people but had a reputation as a group of doing their own thing and not being on the same page. It was a common refrain to hear people say, "I didn't know that's what they were trying to do" or "Why didn't they tell me what they were doing." After setting some very aggressive goals and developing a very detailed plan of attack the general manager held a retreat and asked his people to tell him what they needed to achieve their goals and operate more effectively.

As we facilitated this gathering, a rather interesting thing happened with only a little prompting: these executives developed a specific list of what information they needed from each other and they asked the general manager to be responsible for coordinating the compilation and sharing of this information. They proposed the following:

- A weekly staff meeting limited to thirty minutes to share information (roundtable fashion)
- Electronic distribution of daily and weekly performance activity
- A monthly meeting of all of their staffs in the cafeteria over lunch to talk about what was happening at the organizational level and to answer questions (appropriately labeled "communication meetings")

- The development of an electronic suggestion system and question board run out of the general manager's office
- Greater availability of the general manager to both staff and the employees by holding regular office hours and having a greater presence walking around

These executives in effect developed the general manager's communication system for him based on what they considered to be the current needs of their operation. In about forty-five minutes, they identified the needs, the vehicles, and the frequency of activity. Now it was up to the general manager to do these things and to do them in a value-added fashion—or his credibility would be shot before he ever got off the ground.

■ Practice 4: Nurture Cooperation and Teamwork

IRREFUTABLE PERFORMANCE PRINCIPLE: Effective leadership creates cooperation and teamwork that accelerates the speed at which results can be achieved.

The great Baseball Hall of Famer and former manager of the New York Yankees and Mets Casey Stengel once said, "Getting the players, that's the easy part. . . . Getting them to play together as a team, now that's the hard part." And while Casey Stengel may not have had to deal with the labor shortages of the twenty-first century, every manager can relate to the challenge of getting people to play together as a team. When you find a work unit that is performing at a high level, it is usually no surprise to find people at all levels working together. In our interviews managers frequently used the words *cooperation, collaboration, teaming, pulling together,* and *teamwork* interchangeably to convey the principle that people simply must work together to get results. The real question then becomes, How do managers go about nurturing cooperation and teamwork among the people they need to get results? The answer to this question is very important and addresses a host of issues previously discussed.

Decide the Level of Teamwork Needed

Most managers are given a work unit of people they are responsible for leading to some desired level of performance. After you establish your mission and direction it is important to evaluate and determine the level of cooperation and teamwork that will get the desired results. Sometimes managers are called upon to supervise people whose work does not depend greatly on the efforts of others. A fairly limited category of jobs fall into this category (for example, stockbrokers, some salespeople, certain types of information technology specialists, some maintenance personnel, night security people, and lighthouse keepers). Managers must be highly effective at leading these individuals, but teamwork is not a requisite for achieving desired results.

Usually, however, people in the modern workplace are increasingly dependent on other people to get things done. In fact, the ability to get along with all kinds of people in our culturally diverse workplace was frequently mentioned as being critical for managers and employees alike because of a growing interdependency within organizations. And when people do not work together, a host of performance-busting problems emerge. In some of our earlier research we have found that lack of cooperation and teamwork caused communication breakdowns, inefficiencies, poor customer service, inflated costs, poor productivity or quality, and poor results.

Remove Barriers to Cooperation and Teamwork

Once you've determined the level of teamwork needed, as a manager you must recognize and remove the barriers to cooperation and teamwork that tend to occur without effective leadership.[4] Managers in this study identified a variety of barriers to cooperation and teamwork that can easily defeat any effort to improve performance:

- Lack of unifying goals and direction
- Conflicts arising from different personalities and egos interacting
- Unresolved performance problems and barriers
- Unclear employee roles and responsibilities
- Personal agendas, turf wars, and internal competition
- Rewarding only individual performance
- Communication breakdowns
- Poor planning
- Lack of incentives to work together
- Failing to provide adequate resources

We would like to add one more factor to the list: ineffective leadership, which destroys teamwork and performance. We found that ineffective managers tend to create communication breakdowns, decreased productivity, wasted resources, a degeneration of morale, a loss of coordination, loss of customer focus, increased workplace conflict and political activity, declining profits, and increased stress. Thus, if you are like most managers, you may find that cooperation and teamwork between you and your people is most critical. It has been said that "none of us is as smart as all of us." Let this belief encourage you to take active steps to unlock the power of teamwork in pursuing improved performance and cooperation when you practice effective leadership.

Once you've removed barriers to cooperation and teamwork, you must help your work unit learn to function as a team. When a manager is given a group of people to lead and does lead it effectively, the group tends to develop into a team. A work group is simply a collection of people with a common purpose; a *team*, on the other hand, is a group of people committed to the achievement of specific goals using clearly defined processes with high levels of involvement and cooperation. The hallmark of any great team is teamwork, which is a process that must be understood and stimulated by the role-modeling actions of an effective leader.

Here's an exercise to answer the following question: *As a leader, do you foster cooperation and teamwork among the people you need to get results?*

Find Out Now—Are You Developing Teamwork?

1. Think of a time in your life when you felt like you were part of a team that was getting results.
2. On a piece of paper please list the characteristics that made this team effective.
3. Repeat steps 1 and 2, drawing on your experience as part of a team that was ineffective.
4. Compare and contrast your lists to better understand the factors that cause people to work together as a team both effectively and ineffectively.

If you are like most people who do this exercise, you'll quickly be reminded that most of the characteristics that are part of results-oriented teams are driven by effective leadership practices, many of which have already been discussed.

What's in a Name?

Effective leaders do not confuse *teamwork* with the wide variety of *teams* that have emerged during the past two decades. Self-directed work teams, cross-functional problem-solving teams, customer service teams, empowered production teams, and technology integration teams all abound. Yet calling a group of people a team does not mean that cooperation and teamwork will necessarily follow. In fact, in many organizations the very word *team* breeds cynicism and sarcasm for two reasons. Since teams seem to be in vogue, organizations can have a tendency to loosely label every group of people with a job as "a team." This is a mistake, since these groups are not really teams by definition.

Some organizations turn over work that could or should be done by an individual or "committee of two" to a team of people, which is not an effective use of time or resources. In the words of one manager, "We give work to teams to provide political cover, or because it is popular around here, when lots of these issues could and should have been decided by management or individuals." This particular practice seems to be pervasive these days.

And while certain types of teams can be highly effective in the right environment and application, all teams require leadership and teamwork to mature and develop, and this takes time, effort, and focus. Effective leaders realize that teamwork is not necessarily a goal in itself but rather something that increases the likelihood of desired results when properly stimulated. Thus managers who are serious about improving results take the position that the very practices that promote teamwork are inextricably intertwined with the practices that lead to better performance. The key for a manager therefore is to use effective working relationships, leadership worthy of trust, and effective need-based communication practices to get people to cooperate with each other in meeting goals and objectives.

How to Become a Gateway to Cooperation

It is one thing to know and understand the factors that block teamwork, and quite another to master the practices that unlock the power of cooperation. To this end, leaders must be committed to practices that foster cooperation and teamwork among people. Managers in this study identified a number of key practices that become either *gateways* or *barriers* to cooperation and teamwork based on each leader's effectiveness in dealing with these key actions.

Here's an exercise to answer the following question: *Am I a* gateway *or a* barrier *to cooperation and teamwork?* Take a moment to think about the question first.

Find Out Now—Are You a Gateway to Cooperation?

1. Assess your management of your unit; rate yourself against the criteria in Worksheet 5.3 to see how effective you are in this arena and whether each practice represents a barrier or a gateway to cooperation.

2. Overall, how do your practices stack up? Are you creating more gateways or barriers to cooperation and teamwork in your operation? The answer to this question is critical for obtaining results.

When each of these practices is enacted, it serves as a gateway to teamwork and eventually better performance. When these practices are found to be missing in action, they create barriers that damage work unit performance. Now at this point these practices should be starting to sound redundant. That's because developing 360-degree working relationships, leadership, and communication all draw on many of the same principles. Also, when managers practice the absolutes introduced earlier in this book, it turns out that teamwork is a natural consequence. Thus, we challenge you to master these practices, which can only increase your personal effectiveness and create gateways to better performance and results.

Practical Example—
A Division Vice President's Meaningful Mistake

Several years ago a division vice president named Tonya accidentally signed up for the wrong management education program. She thought she was going to a course on creating customer service teams, but the program actually focused on team-building. She had already made the trip, so she decided to stay. Most of the people in the program were front-line supervisors and middle managers, and the program content was focused on how to get employees to work together. As the first day closed, the seminar leader asked the question, "Do you practice the leadership actions that cause your *employees* to want to work together?" She took this question out of its present context and instead applied it to the managers who worked in her operation: "Do I practice the leadership actions

■ Worksheet 5.3. ■
Getting People to Work Together Assessment: A Baker's Dozen

Key Leadership Practice	Rating	
	Barrier	Gateway
1. My work group has a clearly defined mission understood by all.	☐	☐
2. People have clearly defined roles and performance standards that are understood by others.	☐	☐
3. People are committed to achieving work unit goals.	☐	☐
4. People have the information they need to get their work done.	☐	☐
5. People are kept informed on issues that affect them and have a voice to raise concerns and offer input.	☐	☐
6. We train together as a team.	☐	☐
7. People are actively involved in the planning process.	☐	☐
8. People feel they have input in decision-making and problem-solving processes.	☐	☐
9. People communicate openly with each other and demonstrate trust and integrity.	☐	☐
10. People receive ongoing feedback on both individual and group performance.	☐	☐
11. People have a sense of both ownership and accountability for performance.	☐	☐
12. We meet regularly to address concerns, discuss performance, and remove performance barriers.	☐	☐
13. We celebrate and reward team success.	☐	☐

that cause my *managers* to want to work together?" She admitted to herself that she had called her nine direct reports "a management team" but that in reality they really weren't a team at all. "It became pretty obvious to me, the more I thought about it, that if our employees behaved like my managers, our results would really suffer because cooperation would be replaced by competition."

Upon further reflection she realized that if she wanted more cooperation and teamwork among the division employees, she would need to increase the level of cooperation, and hopefully teamwork, among her managers. In the end, she concluded that she *talked* about teamwork but actually did very few things that caused her people (managers) to cooperate with each other. This approach had damaged performance and set a terrible example for the rest of the workforce. By the end of the two-day program she became convinced that attending this workshop was one of the better mistakes she had made in her career.

CHAPTER SUMMARY

Working relationships, trustworthy leadership, effective communication, and teamwork do not just happen! Building effective working relationships is essential to getting things done in any modern organization because people need each other whether they are willing to admit it or not. Leadership that gets results is always based on a manager's ability to demonstrate actions worthy of employee trust. Without competency and character this trust is called into question. Results-oriented managers are communication centers and therefore are a critical link to the upward, downward, and lateral flow of information which is necessary for success. Finally, successful organizations almost always depend on cooperation and teamwork, which they foster at all levels by effective actions on the part of their managers. These are practices that support the absolute of building effective bridges on the road to better results. These key practices possess the capability of unleashing people power, which is a significant competitive advantage these days. Failing to develop managerial excellence in these areas is a quick way to create potholes on the bridge to better results. These potholes can seriously knock your career off track and make it more difficult than it has to be to come to work and get results.

Absolute #5

Keep the Piano in Tune:
Practice Continuous Renewal

For success and productivity, both organizations and managers need to maintain an ongoing cycle of development.

The CEO of a banking organization aptly described this process to us in these terms: "One of the most exciting and frustrating parts of my job is to keep things moving in the right direction. Just about the time that everything is working well, things change and we've got to make adjustments. It is my job to keep the piano in tune, if you would, so we can make the kind of music our customers and shareholders want to hear. This requires constant adjustments of both our people and systems; otherwise, we'll be in trouble in no time at all."

Preventive Medicine for Health Care

When Gary became president of a large West Coast hospital (which had recently joined a larger health care system), he knew that the organization was in the black, had great people, and had a strong tradition of patient care and medical excellence. What became apparent in fairly short order, though, was the fact that this organization was culturally living in the past. The current health care environment had greatly restricted and capped reimbursements, but this organization had not come to grips with the fact that it was being asked to provide the same level of health care with significantly lower revenues. Costs now needed to be controlled, and processes needed to be redesigned to allow the hospital to maintain high-quality patient care with limited resources.

Current management personnel had, for the most part, come up through the ranks; they lacked some of the critical skills necessary to operate in the new health care industry. And although staff throughout the hospital had tremendous health care acumen, they had only limited experience with empowerment, cost containment, controlling budgets, problem solving, and working in teams. Because of an unwillingness on the part of previous leadership to make some of the difficult decisions required to move this institution in the right direction, Gary found himself running an organization that went from being a health care leader to a health care dinosaur. And now the whole concept of continuous improvement needed to be implemented at both the systems and personnel levels. Gary stated, "While cutting costs and people is gut-wrenching work, getting systems and people aligned with our current needs is the real challenge, one that managers at all levels must be willing and have the courage to meet. We must develop new attitudes, practices, and skills to make a real change in the way we operate."

Had the members of this organization been practicing, from the top down, the absolutes that we have been discussing, this organization would not have reached its current state of crisis. The necessity of keeping the piano in tune so that systems and people are properly aligned to meet current demands takes us to our last set of key results-oriented practices from our study.

■ In Search of Continuous Improvement

It has been said that continuous improvement is both an organizational goal and process, a view we heartily support.[1] Yet managers in our research talk about the concept of development as the key to continuous improvement. *Development* means to grow, evolve, or move something to a more complete, effective, or desirable state. Discussions with managers about improvement almost always focus on "developing the resources you've got to work with," or "developing your people," or "developing yourself," all of which make up our final absolute, renewal (Figure 6.1).

The absolute of renewal means paying attention continuously to four development issues that will allow you to improve

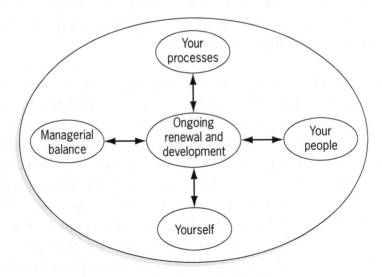

Figure 6.1. Ongoing Renewal and Development for Results

both operational and personal performance. All four issues require change, but—more important—they focus on improvement rather than on change in isolation. Thus, as a results-oriented leader, you can improve the performance of your operation when you make development an ongoing process.

- Work proactively to improve the operating processes that are used for getting things done.
- Determine the importance of employee development, and respond accordingly to help people improve their long-term capabilities.
- Work to improve and refine the skills that are most necessary for you to best lead and support the performance of others.
- Develop and maintain balance around the issues that are most important in your personal and professional life.

■ Practice 1: Develop Improved Processes

IRREFUTABLE PERFORMANCE PRINCIPLE: Effective leaders develop vehicles to proactively improve processes and the factors that influence performance.

Some would argue that if managers are truly interested in improving the overall performance of their operation, they must look for better ways of doing things and for ways to make it easier for people to get things done. So a key technical managerial skill and practice is that of developing more effective and efficient processes. When managers are skilled at removing performance barriers as discussed in Chapter Three, they will inevitably be engaged in some level of process improvement, but a distinction is needed. Problem solving is by definition *reactive*, and although resolving some problems (barriers) can lead to process improvement, managers in this study emphasized the importance of proactively improving processes and systems for getting work done.

It is interesting to note that the Total Quality Management movement of the 1980s and early 1990s got some managers to think about systems and processes. But the reengineering, ISO certifications, Six Sigma, and balanced scorecard movements of late have made documenting, understanding, and improving processes a necessary management practice in many organizations.[2]

A *process* is simply a series of steps, actions, activities, or operations used to bring about a desired result or outcome. Organizations have countless processes—for everything from hiring to ordering supplies to filling customer orders to scheduling work to handling cash. In some organizations, these processes are well thought out, well documented, and properly implemented, and so they tend to help managers and their people get results. In other organizations, many key processes have never been fully developed and are the by-product of tradition, habits, evolution, or "thinking in the box." And they are still in use despite their frequently being neither optimal nor effective. These processes can breed frustration, inefficiencies, and a serious erosion of a manager's credibility. Why? Because the manager is failing to remove a long-term performance barrier or simply not realizing that there are better ways of doing things.

Better Ways of Doing Things

It has been estimated that over two-thirds of all reengineering efforts fail to realize their full potential.[3] A major reason for this lack of success is that the front-line managers whose processes were being redesigned never took ownership of the process, and their people were never made to feel part of the improvement effort. This offers an important lesson: many reengineering efforts fail to take into account the human element necessary to properly implement and sustain such efforts. So it is imperative that managers not only take proactive steps to improve and develop their key operating processes but do so in a fashion that causes their people to take ownership of the changes that follow. This is critical if process-improvement activities are to create actual improvement rather than being viewed simply as frivolous change.

Process improvement can come from any number of sources:

- Employee suggestions
- Benchmarking effective processes and practices in other departments or at other organizations
- Implementing statistical process controls
- Systems reengineering
- Software, equipment, and technology vendor suggestions
- Customer recommendations
- A full-blown process redesign effort

The important points here are that a wide variety of vehicles can be used to create improvement, and that process improvement is critical to improving performance.

Here's an exercise to answer the following question: *Are the most critical processes that we depend on to get results operating in an optimal fashion?*

Find Out Now—Are Your Processes Optimal?

1. Right now, on a blank piece of paper, identify two or three of the processes that are most important to your work unit's performance.
2. Ask yourself the following questions about each of the processes that you've identified:

   Is this process helping us achieve the results we desire?

   Is this process properly documented?

Is this process being followed as designed?

Is this process being systematically measured?

Is the process properly understood by those using it?

Is this process a target for improvement?

3. Based on your answers, determine what needs to be done about that process.

Your conclusions about what to do with the rated processes can fall along a continuum of actions. At one end you might conclude that the process is working well and do nothing. At the other end of the continuum you might conclude that a major process redesign is in order. And in the middle you might conclude that some fine-tuning of the existing process is required to improve performance. Just remember that your processes are the vehicles that people frequently drive on the road to results and they must be in tune with the demands of your current situation.

As you pursue your critical work unit goals and metrics, remember that measurement will be a critical factor in understanding the factors that influence systems performance. It is a well-known business axiom that if you cannot measure something, you cannot control it, and if you cannot control it, you cannot manage it, and if you cannot manage it, you cannot improve it. Thus your measurement systems can be a key source of information to help you both understand the factors or drivers that affect your performance and identify which processes are helping or damaging performance.

Empowering Improvement Teams

A successful executive once said to us, "Not every manager has the time and patience to establish, within their operation, an improvement team to proactively look for ways to make things better. But then again, not all managers are successful either." His comment is a tacit admission that leaders desiring success need to systematically tap into the expertise, creativity, and problem-solving prowess of their employees. And while a manager running a department of five people can develop this proactive practice with the whole staff, a manager with a larger staff—or the director, general manager, or VP—would be well served to create an empowered improvement team for an entire operation. Managers in this study made frequent use of improvement teams as springboards for process improvement.

Our experience in a wide variety of organizations and the input of managers in this study allow us to offer the following guidelines for establishing and developing successful process improvement teams:

- Select team members based on their expertise, credibility, character, chemistry, and direct involvement in the operation.
- Give the team a clear charge—to focus on improvement—and allow them to meet regularly.
- Properly orient and train the team in both group dynamics and the technical, process-oriented skills that are important to proactive improvement and problem solving.
- Empower the team to make decisions, but construct guard rails to keep them from straying into non-improvement or contractual issues that are not their purview.
- Encourage the team to employ effective analytical and process improvement techniques.
- Communicate team activity, recommendations, and actions to managers and employees on a regular basis to keep everyone informed of progress.
- Celebrate success in a timely fashion to reinforce desired outcomes.
- Use team membership as a development tool for employees and managers alike.

As the manager, you might choose to be a member of this team or play a less involved role in the actual meetings. But either way, if this process is to succeed, you must be actively engaged. And the good news is that effective empowered improvement teams have been shown to have a significant impact on performance and process improvement across a wide variety of industries and organizations. In addition, you'll find a myriad of materials, manuals, and resources available to help set up these proactive improvement vehicles. So ask yourself the question, What am I doing in my work unit to proactively improve our processes and performance? The operative word here is *proactively*.

Practical Example—Improving Processes at a Furniture Manufacturer

For the past year, a large furniture-manufacturing operation had been experiencing significant cost increases and production bottlenecks that were driving results into the ground. The organization claimed to be using "empowered production teams," but the problem was twofold: the groups were not empowered, and the people did not work together as a team. And although the plant engineers had streamlined a host of production processes, the integration and coordination of these efforts was seriously lacking. A new plant manager was hired and he immediately created a "process improvement team" made up of workers, supervisors, one engineer, and the plant's operations manager. He gave them a simple charge: *Look for ways of improving performance and making it easier for people to get things done around here.*

After several team-building orientation sessions, the team was unleashed and in short order identified a host of problems that were damaging performance. Some required significant process redesign (for instance, the process for moving work between manufacturing cells). Others required tweaking existing procedures (preventive maintenance). In addition, the team identified specific problems with staffing, training, communications, and production performance feedback, all of which needed to be fixed. The team rotated membership each quarter, and after one year of weekly meetings began to scale back as the operation as a whole improved.

The plant manager stated, "This team was effective, proactive, creative, and cross-functional, and they have had a profound impact. My job was to support them, provide resources, and make sure that the ideas and improvements that we all agreed to got implemented. This is a terrific example of managers and employees working as one." In the end, continuous improvement became a way of life.

■ Practice 2: Perfect the Art of Performance Appraisal

> IRREFUTABLE PERFORMANCE PRINCIPLE: Effective managers practice constructive employee appraisal and development to help their people continuously improve their personal performance.

Results-oriented managers tend to place a great deal of emphasis on their people's development, growth, maturing, and improvement. *Employee development* can be described as efforts to enhance employee skill and performance. This development can be achieved using a host of methods, but it is almost always predicated on the manager having an accurate assessment of an employee's strengths and areas needing improvement as they relate to performance on the job. The most frequent form of assessment discussed by the managers in this research focused on the manager's role as an "appraiser of performance." This role takes place on two levels:

- Ongoing
- Formal

The key term is *constructive appraisal,* which means to use assessment to build others up rather than as a tool to simply control people or tear them down.

Ongoing Performance Appraisal

Ongoing performance appraisal takes place continuously as managers observe employee behavior and performance against key measures and, rather naturally, compare the information they have about the employee against what they consider to be acceptable.[4] For ongoing appraisal to operate in an optimal fashion, managers should always clearly communicate and clarify the employee's performance role and goals and empower the employee for action, as discussed in Chapter Two.

Once this informal appraisal has taken place, effective leaders will use this information as a trigger to provide feedback to the employee and coach the employee to reinforce desired behaviors and change less than-effective-practices. As discussed in Chapter Four, results-oriented leaders make performance management and coaching a priority in their practice of MBWA[3]. Earlier research supports the notion that there is no substitute for a leader who clarifies performance expectations and provides ongoing appraisal, feedback, and coaching. When developed into a manager's daily mode of operation, these actions can have a tremendous motivational effect and impact on performance. And remember, informal appraisal is taking place continuously. So effective leaders use this information to shape employee behavior rather than simply keeping it to themselves. Effective leaders continually look for opportunities to coach and develop their people on the job! This practice can go a long way toward helping people learn on the job and prepare for additional responsibility. In the words of one manager, "Be a leader who is a teacher on a daily basis. Your people will learn, and so will you."

Formal Performance Appraisal

The second type of appraisal is the *formal performance appraisal.* This is an annual or semiannual practice in roughly 90 percent of all U.S. organizations.[5] Organizations typically ask their managers to evaluate their people formally for a host of reasons, including to improve performance planning, to document employee performance, to link merit and pay, and to foster employee development. While managers and employees alike often complain about the process, a detailed study revealed that nearly 70 percent of employees and 80 percent of managers found the appraisal process, when properly conducted, to be beneficial.[6] Why? The formal appraisal process causes certain important things to take place that might not otherwise happen in the heat of battle. When we asked the managers in this study why they conducted formal reviews, the most frequent answer was "because I have to" (as mandated by the organization). Then they went on to describe using the formal appraisal process as an "arena for strategic planning for a business unit of one [the employee]," "a time to look back and learn from the past," "an opportunity to discuss improvement and development," "a time to celebrate success and/or get sober about change," and "a time to wipe the slate clean and start over."

Most managers are expected to do appraisals, so it would behoove us all to learn how to make the process as constructive as possible—especially since it is a litmus test of a manager's effectiveness and trustworthiness as a leader. In a second study, based on the input of several hundred employees, we identified these factors as the primary causes of ineffective formal appraisals:[7]

- The manager does not take the process seriously.
- There are unclear performance standards or subjective ratings.
- The manager has insufficient knowledge of a subordinate's performance.
- There is a lack of ongoing performance feedback.
- The manager lacks sincerity, honesty, and trust.
- The manager is not prepared.
- There is ineffective discussion of employee development.

- The manager lacks skill in doing appraisals.
- There is too much criticism and negativism.
- Unclear and ambiguous language is used.

   This list speaks volumes about the appraisal process as a test of a leader's credibility. These factors quickly come to play when you review the formal appraisal process that most organizations follow (Figure 6.2). Managers must become proficient

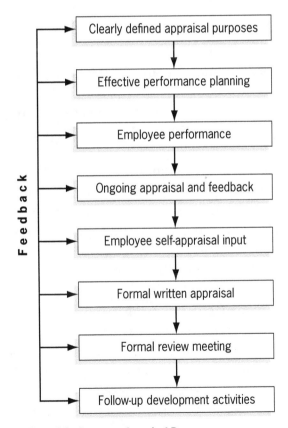

Figure 6.2. The Formal Performance Appraisal Process

at using the formal appraisal process as a constructive activity aimed at helping employees develop.

Results-oriented managers use this formal appraisal process to ensure that they are effectively performing a host of results-oriented practices that can have a significant impact on employee performance, the leader's credibility, and the employee's long-term development. When this process is handled well, good things happen—and the converse is also true.

Here's an exercise to help you answer the following question: *Do you conduct constructive performance appraisals and focus on developing the talents of your people?*

Find Out Now—Are You a Constructive Appraiser?

1. Complete Worksheet 6.1.
2. Note which questions received a response other than "Always."
3. What can you do to integrate these areas into your performance appraisal and employee development practices?

And while it is popular in some circles to talk about doing away with formal appraisals, remember that people want to know where they stand and what they need to do to get better. Performance appraisal can be used to identify specific employee performance needs and to set developmental goals, which need to be crafted into an action plan for improvement and growth. This plan should be the by-product of the employee and the manager's working together to determine how to best accelerate employee learning and performance. The employee must then be given developmental opportunities, which the manager must monitor and follow up on. When this process is a shared responsibility between the manager and employee, it becomes much more than a bureaucratic ritual that has to be performed.

■ Worksheet 6.1. Employee Appraisal and Development ■

Key Issue	Rarely	Sometimes	Always
1. My people clearly understand why we conduct formal appraisals.	☐	☐	☐
2. My people know what they are going to be held accountable for in terms of performance.	☐	☐	☐
3. I monitor employee performance on an ongoing basis.	☐	☐	☐
4. I conduct ongoing appraisals of my people and provide them with both feedback and coaching.	☐	☐	☐
5. I look for opportunities to help my people on the job.	☐	☐	☐
6. I have my people conduct a self-appraisal of their performance to encourage development and ownership	☐	☐	☐
7. My formal written performance reviews focus on providing constructive feedback and specific examples.	☐	☐	☐
8. I take a "no surprise" strategy in performance appraisal discussions and keep things honest and constructive.	☐	☐	☐
9. Once developmental needs are identified we create a plan to improve employee performance.	☐	☐	☐
10. Employee development plans are implemented and regularly reviewed throughout the year	☐	☐	☐

Why Ongoing and Formal
Performance Appraisals Are Important

It is imperative to perfect the art of both ongoing and formal appraisals. Ongoing appraisals are key to ongoing employee performance, improvement, development, and the building of effective working relationships with your people. When ongoing appraisals are effective, employees know that performance is important and that the manager is serious about getting results. This makes accountability for results more of a reality for the employee. A residual effect of strong ongoing appraisals is that a manager is better prepared for conducting constructive formal appraisals that hold no surprises for the employee. The formal appraisal process can thus be used as a vehicle to thoroughly understand how to best help employees improve their performance and to take ownership for results.

Remember that the ongoing and formal appraisal processes represent a needs assessment that can be used to help identify gaps in an employee's ability and underutilization when employee skills are not being put to the best possible use. It must be stated again that when a manager takes a serious interest in an employee's development, the employee's level of commitment and motivation tend to be positively affected. And although the managers in our study spoke often of employee development, that process needs to be visualized.

By using the following guidelines you as a manager can begin to establish more effective development plans with your people:

1. Come to a clear agreement on what functions are most critical to the employee's job and what skills are needed for success.
2. Identify developmental needs of two types:

- Corrective—to fix existing performance problems.
- Growth—to expand and better use an employee's talent.

3. Ask the employee to develop a one- or two-page development plan on how to best enhance their performance, which the manager can review and offer input identifying developmental goals and opportunities.

4. Remember that although people learn by hearing and seeing, they learn mostly by doing, so use appropriate developmental practices. These might include some of the following:
   - Being a mentor
   - Cross-training
   - Job rotation
   - Special assignments
   - Job expansion and additional responsibilities
   - Serving as a coach or trainer
   - Visiting clients or customers
   - Additional formal training and education
   - Peer mentoring
   - Shadowing successful people in the organization to learn what they do and how they do it

Once the development plan has been agreed upon and implemented, follow-up and review are necessary and can take surprisingly little time on the part of the manager. Ongoing appraisal and coaching should be continuously used to evaluate, reinforce, and shape newly acquired skills and behaviors.

Use the formal appraisal process to repeat the development cycle and to reward successful development actions and address areas of concern. Remember that successful development efforts are the shared responsibility of the manager and employee working together in concert to support each other in accomplishing needed changes.

Practical Example—A *Fortune* 500 Manager as Coach

Ramon was a manager with a reputation for developing great people and his department was a way station for people being promoted to other parts of the organization. As the VP of administrative services in a *Fortune* 500 organization, Ramon took great pride in helping his people develop. In fact, his nickname was affectionately "Coach." The CEO of the organization asked Ramon to share his secrets for developing people at an executive retreat. Ramon felt both privileged and humbled to do so. As he began his talk, he told a story of his first boss, who told him, "Son, you are on your own; either get things done or get out." Ramon was thankful to know where he stood, but with time grew to dislike and avoid his results-at-all-costs boss, who wouldn't help him with anything. After eighteen months he decided it was time to go rather than "work for a jerk."

In his second organization, his new boss was a self- proclaimed "developer of people" who became both a coach and mentor to Ramon. As Ramon's skills expanded and his performance drew a lot of attention (which led to his eventual promotion), his boss came to him one day and told him, "Ramon, I need you to tell me what you've learned over the past two-and-a-half years."

Ramon responded, "Everyone needs goals, a plan, and a coach to learn fast."

"And," his boss added, "to use the tools that this company has available to help people grow. Now go help your people like I've helped you."

So Ramon concluded that the secret to growing his people was making employee development his priority, helping employees plan their own development and using the tools and opportunities the organization provided in a meaningful fashion. And he added, "Oh, and by the way, I don't spend more than a few hours each week growing my people, but it is time very well spent that everyone could spare if they really wanted to." When his comments were concluded Ramon thanked the audience and sat down, appreciative of the lessons he'd learned from his boss and coach about how to develop people and the opportunity to share these lessons with others.

■ **Practice 3: Develop a Plan to Improve Your Performance**

IRREFUTABLE PERFORMANCE PRINCIPLE: Effective managers take responsibility for their own development, determining a clear plan of action to improve their current performance and prepare for the future.

A great deal of our discussion about getting results has focused on leaders being people who help other people get things done! Whether it is clarifying, empowering, performance expectations, planning, communicating, equipping, appraising, or coaching, managers must facilitate the performance of others by performing value-added functions. And all managers interested in improving their performance must become adroit at developing the skills that are most necessary to help others succeed. For some managers, this is a significant paradigm shift.

The Realities of Management Development

Although many organizations have very effective processes and programs to help managers improve their performance, managers in this study identified a number of "realities" about management development that support our previous research and should give us all pause:

- Managers receive surprisingly little structured input from their superiors concerning clarifying their value-added role in getting results.
- Managers receive surprisingly little performance feedback and coaching from their superiors on how to improve performance.
- The quality of managerial appraisals is typically less than the subordinate manager desires.

- Management style is rarely discussed short of a crisis.
- Most managers do not have a mentor with whom they regularly meet and build a relationship.
- There is frequently an overreliance on management education and workshops as the primary vehicle for management development.
- Many managers do not have a fully conceived development plan to improve their performance and prepare for their next move.
- Many managers tend to wait on the organization to help them develop their skills and manage their careers.

These realities describe almost to a T similar findings from an article we published in the *Sloan Management Review,* titled "Ten Myths of Managing Managers."[8] It concludes that "managers must take a more proactive role in their development to achieve long-term success because in many cases they are simply not getting the support, input, and direction that they want and need to be effective."

Managers often fall prey to the trap of not placing a priority on their personal development, which can be a career buster. This can happen for a number of reasons:

- They are too busy doing more urgent things.
- They place an overreliance on their boss or their organization for their development.
- They simply don't give their personal development a great deal of thought.
- They believe that they are currently on track to achieve their career goals (which they very well may be), so further development is not a felt need.

Here, a simple caveat must be stated without raising paranoia. With the current pace of environmental and organizational change, all managers must make the improvement of their skills and performance a priority and an ongoing practice. Do not count on your boss or organization, because in the end no one cares about your career development as much as you should and do. No one!

One of the problems with being a manager is that you are so busy that you frequently do not take sufficient time to think about what you are doing and how you are doing it. So here's an exercise to help you answer the following question: *Do you have a real plan to improve your current skills and performance?*

Find Out Now—How Do Other Managers Improve Their Game?

1. Think of four or five managers whom you know and consider to be successful.
2. Select no more than two from your own organization, and get the others from outside your organization (for instance, friends, customers, suppliers).
3. Schedule a 45- to 60-minute meeting with each of them, and ask these fellow managers the following questions:

   What are the greatest challenges you face as manager?

   What are the keys to getting results in your current job?

   What skills are most important to your effectiveness?

   What does your organization do to help you develop as a manager?

   How do you go about improving your performance?

4. If possible, tape record these interviews. Otherwise, write down keyword notes to help you recall the main points. Write down the essence of what you have learned after each interview.

This exercise will help you determine how other managers deal with the same key performance-related issues that you face. In listening to other managers, you will undoubtedly get some ideas about how to improve your own performance. We have found that this exercise is beneficial for managers to realize that they are not alone in their managerial world—a world that instead frequently places a priority on self-reliance, independence, and bravado. By candidly addressing each of these questions, you can learn a number of important things about getting results, including the fact that most other managers are also continuously looking for ways to improve their game. This exercise takes time but it will be time well spent for learning new improvement ideas and expanding your professional networks.

Create Your Development Plan

Remember that when it comes to development, most managers are on their own. If you are like Ramon in the preceding section and have a boss or mentor who is interested in your development, count your blessings! Most managers need to determine their own developmental needs and then create a plan, either on their own or with minimal assistance from their boss. Remember, it all starts with identifying the functions that are most important to getting results and then developing and improving the skills necessary to perform these functions effectively. We would offer managers the following counsel concerning management development, which we have gleaned from a host of managers and organizations over the years:[9]

- Make sure that you clarify an accurate, value-added role that you must serve as a manager to effectively facilitate the performance of others. Develop a plan to improve the skills needed to fulfill this role.
- Constantly monitor your personal performance and the performance metrics of your work unit so you always know where you stand in terms of your performance.

- Seek out 360-degree feedback whenever possible so you know how others perceive your performance. This information can come from both informal and formal feedback systems.
- Work with your boss to make it clear that you want and expect a structured, formal performance review at least once a year so you know where you stand and have an arena in which to discuss your development.
- Develop a one-year and three-year development plan of how you are going to improve your performance and upgrade your skills by specifically identifying needs and developmental opportunities, time lines, and accountabilities for change and improvement.
- Develop a mentoring relationship with someone you trust who is a good listener and wise to the ways of organizational life. That person can provide counsel and emotional support. Meet with them on a regular basis to foster this relationship.
- Seek out opportunities for cross-training and increased contact with customers. Such experiences are valuable learning opportunities and are worth the investment of time as long as they do not prevent you from dealing with more pressing matters.
- Mentor a younger manager and develop an effective relationship so you can maintain empathy and understanding with those you supervise.
- Take advantage of formal training programs to sharpen your skills and get away from the operation or office to refresh and renew yourself. When attending training be an active learner and take steps to implement what you have learned at work by teaching it to others, setting specific implementation goals, and having a peer hold you accountable for implementation.

- Make use of books, videos, audiotapes, self-assessment tools, the growing supply of Web resources, and any other tools that can help foster ongoing learning and growth. (Periodically reviewing and implementing the practices discussed in this book falls into this category.)

Developing yourself is critically important to long-term career success and better results, so make it one of your priorities. You simply must keep your skills in tune with the growing demands of your job to keep your career on track and to help you sleep better at night.

Practical Example—Taking Responsibility for One's Own Development

To illustrate the imperative of development let us return to Karen, the rising star mentioned in Chapter Four, who after five promotions in ten years found the performance of her work group slipping. In an exit interview, she was confronted by a departing employee who told her she did not know how to motivate her people, she was perceived to be overly aggressive, her communication skills were not effective, and she was considered by her staff to be self-centered. Karen was stunned by this revelation but decided to explore the accusations. She had a heart-to-heart talk with her boss, who said, "Karen, you are a little too driven at times, but you know how to get things done," which was a weak endorsement of the concern. She talked to a fellow manager she considered a friend, who told her a little more forcefully, "I know your heart is in the right place, but from where I sit, you are pretty hard on your people." Finally, she left a couple of hours early and went to the public library to ponder the realization that she may not be effectively leading her people and mull over the words of the honest exiting employee, "I think you are better than this." Karen concluded, "I don't think that I would want to work for me!"

She got out a piece of paper and made two lists: (1) things in my job I know I do well and (2) things in my job I need to do better. She came to realize that although she was technically strong across the board, her ability to foster effective working relationships and communicate, coach, motivate, and connect with her staff needed immediate attention. She called back the former staff member and asked for specific recommendations as to what she should do differently. This conversation identified a number of dysfunctional behaviors and the circumstances where they were likely to occur. She started a peer mentoring relationship with a fellow manager, whom she asked to hold her accountable for implementing several specific practices. She also asked her boss to evaluate her progress on a development plan that she created and attached to her formal quarterly performance review. Karen attended a number of executive education programs and read several books on developing more effective interpersonal skills to improve her awareness of the importance of the people side of things.

With time, Karen's skills in these areas improved, and she now humorously describes herself as an "RDM" (a *recovering draconian manager*), a condition she now knows that she must always work to temper and control.

■ Practice 4: Create and Maintain Balance in Your Professional and Personal Life

IRREFUTABLE PERFORMANCE PRINCIPLE: Managers truly interested in long-term success in every area of their lives create and maintain the balance that helps sustain real success.

Managers must be able to create and maintain equilibrium or stability when opposing forces and influences are pushing against them. This means they are able to effectively manage the consequences of these forces and their responses. Some might say that this is simply managing stress, but managing stress is typically reactive, while creating and maintaining balance is again proactive. This is a difficult challenge in today's hyperactive, multitasking, and pressure-filled environment but it is a challenge that must be successfully met.

The Ultimate Balancing Act—Having It All

In this study, managers often talked about the "ultimate balancing act" between their professional lives and their personal lives. Balance is a struggle, especially in a society that tends to glorify professional success while trivializing or demeaning the importance of being a terrific husband or wife, or an awesome parent, or simply taking time to enjoy the fruits of one's labor. It is a well-worn axiom that people today want to "have it all." We all frequently fail to accept that there are physical, mental, and emotional costs associated with having it all and that by attempting to have it all (whatever that means to each one of us), we can find ourselves on a treadmill that prevents us from getting to where we really would like to go both professionally and personally.

To achieve balance between our professional and personal lives requires us to possess the ability to set goals, plan, use resources wisely, make good decisions, and demonstrate discipline. And although many of us apply these principles to our professional life quite well, we do not always develop these same practices in our personal life with the same enthusiasm and vigor. Let's face it, most organizations rarely tell people to go home if they are willing to work into the night and get up and do the same thing tomorrow. So our personal lives frequently have to compete for what is left over when work is done with us (both physically and emotionally). If we do not create a plan to get results with our personal lives and with the people and activities that are truly important to us, we will not be in balance.

An executive in the computer industry was feeling particularly overwhelmed, and said, "I recently had a physical, and my doctor told me to balance my diet to help my blood pressure and cholesterol. My boss tells me to balance the big budget, and I even got new tires the other day that I paid to have balanced. And yet, about the only thing I can't seem to get balanced is my life. I'm running here and there, but I really feel like I'm running in place. And my job is only getting bigger, so I feel kind of like a duck swimming upstream, calm on the outside but paddling frantically under the surface to stay afloat. I feel like short-changing my wife and kids has grown from being an occasional thing to a very bad habit which I feel guilty about. . . . Something must change."

This manager's comments describe many of us—people who are out of balance with their professional and personal lives with the potential for serious long-term consequences.

Why Are We Out of Balance?

Do you have a plan and system to keep your professional and personal life in balance? If not, you need to develop one—and to do so taking into account that a host of personal and professional factors can cause a person to be out of balance for a period of time. You want a plan that will help you build a healthy set of behaviors in both arenas, behaviors that deal with the norm rather than the exception. Review the factors that can cause someone to be out of balance in both arenas and see if you can relate to them:

Professional Life	*Personal Life*
A new job	Marital problems
Lack of resources or support	Loss of a loved one
A major change initiative	Financial difficulties
Politics and turf wars	Drug, alcohol, or gambling problems
A problem employee	
The budgeting process	Pregnancy
End of a performance period	Health problems
Relocating	Birth of a child
Bad boss	Parent problems
Not getting results	Home improvements
Growing responsibilities	Spouse's career changes

These factors can place additional stress on professional and personal life. And if one is struggling to keep things in balance to begin with, these factors can truly cause feelings of being overwhelmed. So if like most people you take work problems home and home problems to work, you should have a real incentive to keep both sides of your life in balance. So why don't people maintain this balance?

We have already discussed the importance of creating a development plan for improving your ability to get results at work. Here's an exercise to help you answer the following question: *Do you have a plan of action to develop and improve balance in your personal as well as your professional life?*

Find Out Now—How's Your Balance?

1. Take a look at the eight areas in Worksheet 6.2, which are the ones managers in our research identified as being important to their personal lives and health.
2. Develop a plan to improve your personal life by identifying specific improvement goals, activities, and accountabilities in each of these areas. Use Worksheet 6.2 to help you. Keep your plan simple and focus on the areas that will help you get better balance in your personal life.
3. You may also consider doing this with your significant other.

Do you work to live or do you live to work? How you handle the development and implementation of creating balance and getting better results in your personal life will speak volumes about this issue.

Managers made it clear that without time, effort, planning, and commitment, their personal lives in general, and their families in particular, would be short changed! But know this: people who are paid to get results at work have great tools that can be applied to also getting results in their personal lives when

---

■ Worksheet 6.2. Developing a Personal Life ■

Key Dimensions	Improvement Goals	Activity	Accountability
1. Marriage and relationships			
2. Improved parenting			
3. Social life			
4. Physical health			
5. Intellectual development			
6. Relaxation			
7. Hobbies and interests			
8. Spiritual			

---

they apply them with due care. If your personal life is truly a priority, you can make it work as well as your professional life.

The second primary area of balance that emerged in this research was a manager's ability to find balance in professional life along four key dimensions. Ask yourself each of the following questions and think through your response:

Do I balance being busy versus being effective?
Do I balance my concern for people versus my concern for tasks?
Do I balance short-term versus long-term thinking and behavior?
Do I balance my personal needs versus the needs of others?

When approaching your work, remember that the urgent is seldom important, and the important is seldom urgent. *Important* management practices like planning, coaching, problem-solving, team-building, training and ongoing appraisal can be pushed aside for more *urgent* managerial activities like meetings, paperwork, meetings, budgeting, meetings, e-mail exchanges, meetings, reports, and even more meetings. Results-oriented managers balance both sets of concerns by realizing that an exclusive focus on the short term can damage long-term results and vice versa. We are all busy people, but are we effective? This will be determined by our ability to enact a value-added set of behaviors that facilitate the work of others. Remember that you are not being paid to be busy; you are being paid to get results by your actions. Thus, once your value-added role is determined, you must take the time and have the discipline to do the right things and do them well.

When balancing people versus tasks, know yourself, and realize that to get desired results a dual focus is almost always needed. A focus on either extreme can be a career buster. Keep in mind that the significant majority of results-oriented practices are driven by the *people* components of communication, empowerment, leadership, working relationships, teamwork, training, staffing, development, and the like. If you are a manager who is more task oriented than people oriented, some soul-searching is in order, for ultimately you get results with people. Balance on this particular dimension is critical to creating a high-performance operation that can change and adapt rapidly. Remember, you can't do it all by yourself.

Finally, remember to balance personal needs with the needs of others. While your personal work is critical and personal achievements and rewards are important, you are ultimately being paid to help others get results and feel a sense of achievement. Those who focus only on satisfying their own needs and ego find a myriad of problems close behind. Managers can ill-afford to be labeled egocentric, arrogant, selfish, greedy, pleased with themselves, or jerks. All these personality traits turn people off and limit their ability to have a lasting positive impact on the people they need to get results. In the end, it becomes crucial that a manager develop awareness and sensitivity for each of these important dimensions of balance to achieve meaningful long-term effectiveness.

Practical Example—A Wake-up Call for Balance

It was a wake-up call, although he didn't know it at the time. Stan was working at his desk at about 6:30 P.M., pushing to get out the door late for his daughter's game and feeling stressed out when "it" happened. He woke up at 2 A.M. staring through the oxygen mask at the ceiling and lights of his hospital room, wondering what had happened. His wife rose from her bedside chair and took his hand, saying, "Stan, you had a heart attack, but the doctor says you are going to be OK." "You are young and strong," the nurse added. Stan thought, "I don't feel young or strong. I'm forty-five years old, and I just had a heart attack."

Stan had been working a legitimate sixty-plus-hour workweek for months to bring a new computer system online. In his own words he'd been "overeating," "drinking too much coffee," "getting too little sleep," and "not exercising." He was still working hard to be a good husband and father, and although his heart was there, the time just wasn't available. Stan's life had become a whirlwind of constant task-oriented motion, and his implementation team members agreed that "his management style was pretty helter-skelter because he didn't take time to plan, communicate, and delegate very well. Although he was extremely busy he wasn't very effective."

During his recovery, Stan realized that his lack of balance had nearly killed him. His doctor monitored his work schedule for the next several months. He did a lot of soul-searching and realized that some significant changes were in order. Stan was a principled, educated, and hard-working man who had allowed his life to spin out of balance and control. In our interview with him, he shared something profound and worth remembering, "If this could happen to me it could happen to anybody who allows work to take control of their life!" Stan was right, and he was very grateful for his wake-up call and for the opportunity to change and regain the balance necessary for real success both at work and home.

CHAPTER SUMMARY

It has been said that "bad habits develop a day at a time and are broken a year at a time," which is undoubtedly true for most people. If an organization and its members do not break bad or dysfunctional organizational habits and practices they will quickly go out of tune. Managers must make renewal and development a way of life if they are truly desirous of better performance.

Developing and improving processes and people is essential for long-term success. Developing yourself as a manager just might be the key to every other management practice that we have discussed in this book.

And finally, developing balance in both one's professional and personal life helps a manager stay in tune for true long-term results and career success. Remember that time on the job affects time off the job (and vice versa), so it behooves all of us to develop better balance in our life as a whole. This cannot happen unless we are willing to develop our people, to harness their energy and talent, to refine our processes to make it easier to get work done and, most important, to develop ourselves so that we can be more attuned to doing the right things, the right way, at the right time.

Afterword

The Call for Action

S ocrates once said, "The challenges of life mandate that we apply all our wisdom to daily situations lest we fall prey to our own folly." This seems an appropriate thought as we close this book. The modern marketplace is a very competitive and unforgiving place. The challenges of that marketplace require organizations and managers to apply all of their wisdom (useful knowledge and experience) to the way they run their organization or they will fall victim to their own folly (foolishness). To support this contention, Dun and Bradstreet, which tracks business failures, used to ask why a business failed. "But we discontinued those surveys because the reasons were very stable," said Joe Derwean, Dun and Bradstreet's chief economic adviser. *"Ninety percent of failures are the result of bad management."* And there are a lot of ineffective managers around these days causing business failures because they fail to apply all their accumulated knowledge and experience to the way they operate on a daily basis.

■ Life Is Tough, But . . .

John Wayne, the famous American actor, mirrored Socrates' view two millennia later when he said, "Life is tough, but it is tougher if you are stupid." Organizations and managers are *ignorant* if they do not know what to do to be successful. But they are stupid if they know what to do and for whatever reason fail to do it! We say this not to be offensive but to make it clear that we can all do stupid things when we do not apply what we know to be true. And when managers do stupid things the cost is very high. It is our contention that many organizations and managers do the things that lead to failure not because they do not know what to do, but rather because of organizational and individual inertia they are unable to break bad habits or focus their energies to create and implement a plan to improve. This in turn makes organizational life tougher than it has to be for everyone.

One of the major challenges that managers face in attempting to improve and get things right is that they are constantly bombarded with a variety of "hot practices" that they are told they should implement. Many of these practices are frequently labeled as fads. They are popular for a while and get a lot of attention, but then they fall from grace and just sort of disappear. This endless procession of hot practices frequently causes managers to lose credibility with people and while simultaneously providing cartoonist Scott Adams's "Dilbert" with an unlimited supply of examples of management folly and organizational nonsense. Recent examples of these hot management practices can be filled in using the following sentence. "Managers can *achieve excellent performance* if they will simply . . . !"

- Set stretch goals
- Become coaches to their employees
- Practice open-book management
- Reengineer their processes
- Become facilitators
- Develop and employ work teams
- Become situational leaders
- Practice continuous improvement
- Empower their people
- Pay for performance
- Become change agents
- Get ISO certified
- Manage their metrics

The problem is not that these practices are ineffective at improving long-term performance. Rather, the problem lies with the fact that managers do not approach the demand for improving performance and adopting these practices with an overall passion, commitment, and game plan to effectively employ these proven practices in a complete, ongoing, and systematic fashion. Stop right now and think of the best manager with whom you have ever had the privilege of working. Make a list on a piece of paper of the specific things that made them "the best." In all likelihood they employed most of the absolutes discussed in this book as part of their organizational lifestyle with great effect (as opposed to using them in isolation as fads). Great management practices are only fads if they are whimsically used for a short time and then simply discarded or forgotten. When you find a manager who is struggling to improve or whose results are suffering you will often find a manager who is failing to practice the absolutes necessary for achieving success in a consistent, complete, and ongoing fashion.

All organizations want and need better performance—and that requires managers who know *how* to get results. Yet there is a huge gap between knowing what to do and doing it. This point is made quite evident in the following observation made by a Midwest plant manager:

> Every organization in this country wants to improve its bottom line and operating results. . . . But from a manager's perspective, there is a huge difference between wanting to change and get better and actually having the skill, discipline, and, if I can say, courage to do it. . . . I've worked for five different organizations during my thirty-year career, and I know that only a handful of managers are truly masters at making things better and improving their operations in a systematic fashion. Those are the ones that have a system, know themselves, and practice great fundamentals across the board. . . . In the global marketplace, improving your ability to get results isn't just important, it is an imperative to keeping your job.

The absolutes for getting improved long-term results we have discussed in this book have four things in common: they are timeless; they address a host of critical interrelated needs necessary for effective performance; they are controllable factors that can be influenced by the actions and behaviors of individual managers; and they must be practiced with diligence, commitment, and passion on an ongoing basis.

The great head coach Vince Lombardi, of the world champion Green Bay Packers, would start each season's training camp by holding up a football and stating, "Gentlemen, this is a football." This may have been insulting to some veterans, but it underscored his commitment to starting with basics and to mastering the fundamentals of the game. He would then add, "If we can run, block, tackle, throw, and catch better than our opponents we will win!" Again his emphasis targeted the fundamental practices necessary to compete and be successful. The same sentiment has been shared by former Chrysler CEO Lee Iacocca, who said, "When I leave, I guess my only legacy will be left on the walls, my commandments of management—my distillation of forty-four years in the business world . . . most importantly, "Remember the fundamentals."

■ The Time Is Now

Several years ago we were conducting a weeklong management education program for a division in a *Fortune* 500 manufacturing organization that was (and still is) experiencing huge competitive pressure. At the end of the last day, a well-educated and very sharp thirty-five-year-old manager asked if we had a few minutes to talk. So we all sat down in a corner of the now-deserted conference room. Over the course of the next hour this manager went on to describe how his performance had fallen off over the past twelve months, how he was in the doghouse with his boss, how he was shortchanging his people in terms of his time, and how he was putting in too many hours at work, a practice that was causing tension at home. He stated, "I feel like a failure because of what is happening at work, and this program really made me feel worse because I am not doing most of the things we have discussed [which happen to have been most of the absolutes discussed in this book]. . . . What do you guys think I should do?"

Our response was aimed at getting him to take charge of his situation as we said, "What do *you* think you should do to improve your performance and take control of your situation?" He asked for a few minutes to take a couple of notes. He then returned with three questions written on a piece of paper:

- What results are really needed for my operation to be successful?
- What specific practices do I need to implement to help my operation get desired results?
- Do I currently have the skills necessary to make these practices effective?

We were very impressed with the clarity of both his questions and his response when he said, "I really need to answer these questions for myself before I can develop a plan of attack to get out of this mess I'm in." And as we watched this manager turn his performance around over the course of the next several months, we remained impressed with the power and simplicity of his approach. He realized that he needed to address each of these questions in a very systematic fashion and focus his energies on fundamentals even as his world was becoming more and more complex. The key that we have seen work for managers time and time again is the ability to make the complex and complicated process of managing and leading as simple as possible.

So if you are truly interested in improving your performance to get better results, you must be passionately committed to developing a plan of attack that focuses on improving your fundamentals. To this end, let us share with you a critical way of thinking about improving your performance based on the three questions the manager raised. This way of thinking encompasses all the absolutes covered in this book and will help you visualize how to get the ball rolling to become better at what you do as a manager:

1. *Always start with the end in mind.* Identify the kind and level of results you and your people need to be successful. As we have discussed, determining where you are going is critical in determining how you are going to get there. *You must clarify the right*

results that add value to your organization to be effective as a leader. To not do so is to make life hard for yourself and your people.

2. *Build a model of the absolutes that are most critical to getting the results that are needed.* Once desired results have been clearly established, your job as a results-oriented manager is to identify and build a business model of the practices that are absolutely necessary for success. The absolutes discussed in this book are what a sample of over two thousand high-performance managers saw as critical to their success. These practices are most likely critical to your success as well, but you must build a model of the practices that are most appropriate for your current situation. Stop right now and complete the Getting Results Assessment a second time—presented as Worksheet 7.1 for your convenience—and see how your view of these practices has changed after reading this book.

3. *Identify the practices that are most critical to your success.* Use these to construct a model for high performance that you must implement and perfect. You must identify and implement the right practices to get results that are needed and expected. Now ask yourself a simple question: What happens to performance if I do not implement these practices effectively? Your answer should motivate you to do the right things and to do them well.

4. *Develop the talents needed to implement and sustain the absolutes for high performance.* Finally, you must identify your strengths and areas needing improvement in terms of the knowledge, skills, and attitude that are necessary for better performance. Your effectiveness in implementing the absolutes will be determined to a great extent by your knowledge, skills, and attitudes. A personal development plan to improve in these areas is critically important, as we discussed in Chapter Six. Remember, do not wait for other people to help you develop your talents. You must take charge of the process of developing the talents you need to be successful and you must do so with due care.

■ Worksheet 7.1. ■
Getting Results Assessment

Instructions: Answer each of the following questions in an honest and open fashion to assess the extent to which you are effectively engaged in the practices that lead to improving performance and results. Use the following rating scale:

1=Never   2=Rarely   3=Sometimes   4=To a Great Extent   5=Always

To What Extent Do I . . .

1. Practice effective communications to understand others and to be understood? _____

2. Lead by example and demonstrate competency and character in the workplace? _____

3. Have a clear vision and mission for where I am leading my people? _____

4. Hold people accountable and motivate them to increase their performance? _____

5. Clarify performance expectations with all my employees? _____

6. Foster cooperation and teamwork with the people who need each other to get results? _____

7. Use clearly defined and balanced performance metrics to measure performance? _____

8. Work at continually developing and nurturing key working relationships? _____

9. Ensure that my people are properly trained and educated to get results? _____

10. Employ appropriate and systematic planning practices? _____

■ Worksheet 7.1. ■
Getting Results Assessment, Cont'd

11. Work to rapidly remove performance barriers that get in
    the way of getting results? _____

12. Keep myself up-to-date with the skills necessary to be
    effective in my job? _____

13. Provide ongoing performance feedback and coaching to
    my people? _____

14. Take extreme care in staffing the operation? _____

15. Proactively clarify my value-added organizational role? _____

16. Regularly monitor and measure the operation's
    performance? _____

17. Work to make sure that people are properly equipped to
    perform their jobs? _____

18. Have mechanisms in place to improve processes on an
    ongoing basis? _____

19. Constructively appraise my employees' performance and
    establish plans for their development? _____

20. Work to maintain balance in all facets of my life? _____

Interpretation: Any practice that receives less than a score of 4 is a potential target behavior for improving your personal performance and
propensity for getting better results.

So answer each of these questions honestly for yourself:

- Do I have a clear and unambiguous picture of what results are needed to be successful?
- Have I created and implemented a model of the absolutes that are most needed for success in our operation?
- Do I currently have the skills and knowledge I need to make these practices effective?

Your ability to answer and respond to each of these questions is critical to your long-term career success and survival. Failing to systematically address these critical issues will not only greatly limit your ability to achieve higher levels of performance but will also make your work life tougher than it has to be. Thoreau once said, "This time, like all time, is a great time, if we simply know what to do with it." Please remember this thought as you develop your plan of attack to become the results-oriented manager that you are capable of becoming!

Notes

Chapter One

1. Jack L. Simonetti, "Key Pieces of the Career Survival and Success Puzzle," *Career Development International* 4 (June 1999): 312–317.
2. C. O. Longenecker and T. C. Stansfield, "Why Plant Managers Fail: Causes and Consequences," *Industrial Management* (January-February 2000): 24–32.
3. Robert A. Portnoy, *Leadership: Four Competencies for Success* (Upper Saddle River, N.J.: Prentice Hall, 1999).

Chapter Two

1. C. O. Longenecker, J. L. Simonetti, and T. W. Sharkey, "Why Organizations Fail: The View from the Front-Line," *Management Decision Journal* 37 (1999): 503–513.
2. Michael Treacy and Fred Wiersema, "How Market Leaders Keep Their Edge," *Fortune* (February 6, 1995): 88–98.
3. Noel M. Tichy and Stratford Sherman, *Control Your Destiny or Someone Else Will: Lessons in Mastering Change—The Principles Jack Welch Is Using to Revolutionize General Electric* (New York: Harper-Business, 1994).

4. Peter F. Drucker, *Managing for Results* (New York: HarperCollins, 1964); Stephen P. Robbins and David A. Decenzo, *Fundamentals of Management: Essential Concepts and Applications* (Upper Saddle River, N.J.: Prentice Hall, 2001).

5. Robert S. Kaplan and David P. Norton, "Using the Balanced Scorecard as a Strategic Management System," *Harvard Business Review* (January-February 1996): 75–85, 173; Scott MacStravic, "A Really Balanced Scorecard," *Health Forum Journal* (May-June 1999): 64–67; Robert S. Kaplan and David P. Norton, "The Balanced Scorecard—Measures That Drive Performance," *Harvard Business Review* (January-February 1992): 71–79.

6. Douglas McGregor, *The Human Side of Enterprise* (New York: McGraw-Hill, 1960).

7. Clinton O. Longenecker, "The Delegation Dilemma," *Supervision* (February 1991): 3–5.

Chapter Three

1. Alan A. McLean, *Work Stress* (Reading, Mass.: Addison-Wesley, 1979); James C. Quick and Jonathan D. Quick, *Organizational Stress and Preventive Management* (New York: McGraw-Hill, 1984); Susan Fritz, F. William Brown, Joyce Povlacs Lunde, and Elizabeth A. Banset, *Interpersonal Skills for Leadership* (Upper Saddle River, N.J.: Prentice Hall, 1999).

2. C. O. Longenecker, D. J. Dwyer, and T. C. Stansfield, "Barriers and Gateways to Workforce Productivity: Lessons to Be Learned," *Industrial Management* (April—March 1998): 21–28.

3. Jeffrey Pfeffer and John F. Veiga, "Putting People First for Organizational Success," *Academy of Management Executive* 13 (1999): 37–48.

4. R. Wayne Mondy and Robert M. Noe, *Human Resource Management* (Upper Saddle River, N.J.: Prentice Hall, 1996).

5. R. R. Reilly and W. R. Manese, "The Validation of a Mini-Course for Telephone Company Switching Technicians," *Journal of Applied Psychology* 32 (1979): 83–90.

6. C. O. Longenecker, "The Consequences and Causes of Ineffective Organizational Training Practices," *HR Advisor* (November-December 1997): 5–13.

7. Jack Stack and Bo Burlingham, *The Great Game of Business* (New York: Currency Doubleday, 1992); John Case, *Open-Book Management: The Coming Business Revolution* (New York: HarperBusiness, 1995).
8. D. Lahote, J. L. Simonetti, and C. O. Longenecker, "Management Training and Development at Aeroquip-Vickers: A Systems Approach, Part I," *Industrial and Commercial Training* 31 (1999): 132–135; D. Lahote, J. L. Simonetti, and C. O. Longenecker, "Management Training and Development at Aeroquip-Vickers: A Systems Approach, Part II," *Industrial and Commercial Training* 31 (1999): 213–218.

Chapter Four

1. Don Shula and Ken Blanchard, *Everyone's a Coach: You Can Inspire Anyone to Be a Winner* (New York: HarperBusiness, 1995).
2. C. O. Longenecker, T. C. Stansfield, and D. J. Dwyer, "The Human Side of Manufacturing Improvement," *Business Horizon* (March-April 1997): 7–17; C. O. Longenecker and G. Pinkel, "Coaching to Win at Work," *Manage* (January-February 1997): 19–21.
3. C. O. Longenecker and J. A. Scazzero, "The Ongoing Challenge of Total Quality Management," *Total Quality Management* 8 (1996): 55–60; C. O. Longenecker and J. A. Scazzero, "Improving Service Quality: A Tale of Two Operations," *Managing Service Quality* 10 (2000): 227–232.

Chapter Five

1. Dave Ulrich, Jack Zenger, and Norm Smallwood, *Results-Based Leadership: How Leaders Build the Business and Improve the Bottom Line* (Cambridge, Mass.: Harvard Business School Press, 1999).
2. Daniel Goleman, "Leadership That Gets Results," *Harvard Business Review* (March—April 2000): 78–90.
3. Stephen R. Covey, *Principle-Centered Leadership* (New York: Fireside Books, Simon & Schuster, 1990).
4. Clinton O. Longenecker and Mitchell Neubert, "Barriers and Gateways to Management Cooperation and Teamwork," *Business Horizons* (September-October 2000): 37–44; Carla Joinson, "Teams at Work,"

HR Magazine (May 1999): 30—36; Allan B. Drexler and Russ Forrester, "Interdependence: The Crux of Teamwork," *HR Magazine* (September 1998): 52–62.

Chapter Six

1. C. O. Longenecker, J. A. Scazzero, and T. T. Stansfield, "Quality Improvement Through Team Goal Setting, Feedback, and Problem Solving: A Field Experiment," *International Journal of Quality and Reliability Management* 7 (1994): 45–52.
2. H. James Harrington, *The Improvement Process: How America's Leading Companies Improve Quality* (New York: McGraw-Hill, 1987); Jac Fitz-Enz, *The Eight Practices of Exceptional Companies: How Great Organizations Make the Most of Their Human Assets* (New York: American Management Association, 1997).
3. Peter R. Scholtes, *The Leader's Handbook: Making Things Happen, Getting Things Done* (New York: McGraw-Hill, 1998).
4. C. O. Longenecker, "Why Managerial Performance Appraisals Are Ineffective: Causes and Lessons," *Career Development International* 2 (1997): 212–218.
5. Clinton O. Longenecker and Laurence S. Fink, "Creating Effective Performance Appraisals," *Industrial Management* (September-October 1999): 18–23.
6. Clinton O. Longenecker and Stephen J. Goff, "Performance Appraisal Effectiveness: A Matter of Perspective," *SAM Advanced Management Journal* (Spring 1992): 17–22.
7. Clinton O. Longenecker and Stephen J. Goff, "Why Performance Appraisals Still Fail," *Journal of Compensation and Benefits* (November-December 1990): 36–41.
8. Clinton O. Longenecker and Dennis A. Gioia, "SMR Forum: Ten Myths of Managing Managers," *Sloan Management Review* (Fall 1991): 81–90.
9. C. O. Longenecker and L. S. Fink, "Improving Management Performance in Rapidly Changing Organizations," *Journal of Management Development* 19 (2000).

The Authors

Clinton O. Longenecker is the Stranahan Distinguished Professor of Management in the College of Business Administration at the University of Toledo. His teaching and research focus on leadership, human resource management, organizational development, and common sense solutions to organizational problems. Dr. Longenecker has published over eighty journal articles, and his research results appear in a wide variety of practitioner and academic publications, including the *Sloan Management Review,* the *Academy of Management Executive, Organizational Dynamics, The Journal of Business Ethics, Strategic Decision, Business Horizons,* and *The Wall Street Journal.* During his academic career, he has received seven awards for excellence in teaching and research. He has extensive international business experience; he has worked in both public and private sectors in Russia, Poland, Hungary, Barbados, Haiti, and Zimbabwe.

Dr. Longenecker is an active management consultant, trainer, and executive coach, whose clients include a wide variety of *Fortune* 1000 manufacturing and service organizations as well as entrepreneurial and start-up enterprises. He and his coauthor, Jack Simonetti, frequently team teach management education programs throughout the United States. They have been described as "two of the most dynamic and insightful seminar leaders to be found anywhere." Dr. Longenecker also is an instructor in the Executive Education Program at the University of Michigan Business School, he sits on the board of directors of a number of organizations, and he is an active community servant.

In 1984, Longenecker earned his Ph.D. degree in organizational behavior from the Pennsylvania State University. He has an MBA degree (1978) in management and a BBA degree (1977) in marketing, both from the University of Toledo, where Jack Simonetti was his teacher and mentor. Dr. Longenecker's e-mail address is clinton.longenecker@utoledo.edu.

Jack L. Simonetti has been an adjunct professor of executive education at the University of Michigan Business School since 1980. Dr. Simonetti also is professor emeritus of management at the University of Toledo, where he received a number of outstanding teaching awards during his distinguished career. In 2000, he was honored by the University of Toledo's College of Business Administration with the creation of the Jack Simonetti Graduate Teaching Award to recognize graduate teaching excellence at the College. Dr. Simonetti's teaching and research interests include human resource management, leadership, teamwork, and organizational change. He has published more than 100 articles in leading management and business journals, both in the United States and abroad, and his research has been cited in a variety of sources. Dr. Simonetti also is the coauthor of another UMBS series book, *Strategic Interviewing: How to Hire Good People.*

Prior to his academic career, Simonetti gained extensive industrial experience in his work with the BF Goodrich Company, where he was responsible for a variety of human resource management and employee relations functions. He also has gained extensive consulting and executive education experience through working with a wide variety of U.S. and foreign public- and private-sector organizations. Dr. Simonetti currently is involved in a groundbreaking, e-learning joint venture between the University of Michigan Business School and the London Financial Times Knowledge Company in creating a CD-ROM e-learning tool called "Developing the Manager in You."

In 1972, Simonetti earned his doctoral degree in management from Kent State University. He has an MBA degree (1966) in management from Indiana University and a BS degree (1965) in industrial management from the University of Akron. His e-mail address is simoform@aol.com.

The authors encourage readers to share their real-life examples of organizations and managers who are getting results using the practices described in this book via e-mail.

Index

CPSIA information can be obtained
at www.ICGtesting.com
Printed in the USA
FSHW011738291119
64523FS